04/90

Shadows on the Tundra

Alaskan Tales
of Predator, Prey, and Man

Tom Walker

Stackpole Books

Copyright © 1990 by Tom Walker

Published by
STACKPOLE BOOKS
Cameron and Kelker Streets
P.O. Box 1831
Harrisburg, PA 17105

Printed in the United States of America

10 9 8 7 6 5 4 3 2 1

First Edition

Cartographer: Donna Gates King

Delta Autumn, from *Go Down Moses* © 1942 by William Faulkner. Used with the permission of
Random House Inc., 201 East 50th Street, New York, NY 10022.

Rime of the Ancient Mariner, from *Harper Anthology of Poetry*, John F. Nims, Editor © 1981 by Harper
and Row. Used with the permission of Harper and Row Inc., 10 East 53rd Street, New York, NY
10022.

Bear Attacks © 1985 by Stephen Herrero. Used with the permission of the publisher, Nick Lyons
Books, 31 West 21st Street, New York, NY 10010.

Library of Congress Cataloging-in-Publication Data

Walker, Tom, 1945–
    Shadows on the tundra : Alaskan tales of predator, prey, and man /
Tom Walker. – 1st ed.
        p. cm.
    ISBN 0-8117-1724-0
    1. Hunting – Alaska. 2. Game and game birds – Alaska. I. Title.
SK49.W35 1990
799.29798 – dc20   89-35592
                                                           CIP

For V.W. and J.W.

CONTENTS

FOREWORD

Tom Walker and I have said hello but aren't tested friends, not yet. I haven't faced the ninth rainy morning on a bellyful of his porridge, nor has he tried to survive my snoring. Somehow, though, there is a kinship. A dream of the northwoods sucked him out of a California suburb in 1966 in the same mysterious way one had drawn me from the crowded shores of Narragansett Bay ten years before. Like Tom, I've felt the fierce charge of adrenalin that pushes the bullet toward the quarry change almost instantly to the flooding sadness that brings you to a bewildered half-numbed stand over the life you've just snuffed out. I even have my grizzly stories, thanks to a Labrador retriever who forgot that only ptarmigan should be brought back out of the willows.

There are big differences between us, of course. One is that, while I play at it, Tom is a real outdoorsperson. Authenticity resonates in every line of his writing. When you read that a pleasant jaunt has, suddenly and in spite of the skilled care of every previous step, become a touch-and-go question of survival—that's the way it was. No dramatic embellishments to please an editor or magnify the author. The drama is inherent in every wrinkle of the wild northern landscape, every sudden squall, every twist of the game trail.

And oh, how Tom Walker loves that country and its creatures! Once, years back, it probably was a romantic infatuation, springing from a deep and powerful place in his psyche but without the grounding of knowledge or experience. Now and long since, that feeling has steadied, rooted, ripened. It is his lodestar, his dynamo, the referent for his own self-judgment. You can sense the question always there in his mind: Did I match up that time? Was I alert enough, skilled enough, courageous enough, gentle enough, sensitive enough? After the rifle discharged the bullet, did I discharge my responsibilities to the crippled running beast who must be found, or to the clean kill, which must be given the necessary respect of skilled and thrifty butchering? Perhaps one person in a hundred can love the land well enough to drink in its pungence, its feel, its music, its beauty. Perhaps one in a thousand can, like Tom Walker, ask what it is that he can give in return. And keep on until he finds an answer.

No one who has that kind of relation to the North can avoid anxious, even anguished, hours of thought about the future of its wildlife. Tom has paid his dues in that respect, and his shared campfire reflections occasionally alight on one or another of today's worrisome issues of wild animal and wild land conservation. Yet, in this book, these are only a secondary theme. You can guess that Tom is less happy thinking of habitat and populations in an abstract, statistical way, than as particular places and individuals he has encountered. You can guess, too, that Tom must face every prospect of taking sides in adversary politics with some reluctance, even if in the end he does it.

The main theme, however, is the interaction of a single person with very real and specific pieces of country. One on one, nothing held back, no questions ducked. This relationship, for Walker, is repeatedly concentrated into the extraordinary moment when eyes of the man and the animal meet. A trapped wolf, for instance, lies with its head between its forepaws as the trapper Tom is accompanying walks to it, pistol in hand; and its unwavering gaze relentlessly crucifies its captors on the turmoil of their own emotions. Inevitably you have to recall Aldo Leopold's experience—a near-religious conversion, it would be fair to say—when he saw the green fire die in the eyes of the wolf he had killed on that New Mexican mountain.

Tom, his writing, and the country of his living all seem to be of a piece. Lean but strong, nothing unnecessary. Quiet. Evocative. Enduring. Honest, but not everything revealed at once, unsought or unearned. Possessed of knowledge and of something beyond knowing which must, in the last analysis, be called love.

Robert B. Weeden
Professor, University of Alaska–Fairbanks

ACKNOWLEDGMENTS

This book may be autobiographical in nature, but it attempts much more. Many people have provided assistance, review, and criticism. Biologists Lyman Nichols, Jim Rearden, and Sterling Miller gave freely of their professional expertise, as did Katherine Jope and Derek Stonorov. Professional papers provided by the Alaska Department of Fish and Game, University of Alaska, and the Pratt Museum also aided in the project, specifically the professional reports of biologists Julius Reynolds, Victor Van Ballenberghe, Patrick Valkenberg, William Gassaway, Jim Davis, Harry Reynolds, John Schoen, Robert Stephenson, and Warren Ballard. Bud Branham and John Hewitt added important details to their character vignettes. Writers Peg Peoples, Nancy Lord, and Tom Gresham patiently read and critiqued various passages and offered suggestions. To all, and others, thank you.

INTRODUCTION

Although primarily about hunting, this book is for everyone concerned with Alaska's wildlife and wildlands.

On the subject of hunting there is no neutral ground. Nothing, it seems, arouses such conflicting passions as this ancient and once universally honored pursuit. There are many rationales why humans hunt in a time when wild animals rarely serve as a primary food source. Some hunters will say it's to maintain the balance of nature; their opponents contend that it's just for the pleasure of killing. Both positions are extreme.

In Alaska, as in some western states and Canadian provinces and territories, there are people, both aboriginals and newcomers, whose quality of life is tied to hunting and wildlife. Perhaps the days when people hunted to live have passed, but there are still people who live to hunt. Some people—rural and urban—live very close to the country and depend on it for both spiritual and physical sustenance. Modern hunting, with all its ambiguities and contradictions, has a venerable tradition based in primordial ritual. Some hunters find the tradition debased and anachronistic but no less an integral part of life. Some of them strive not only for an increased quality of experience but understanding as well.

I offer no profound explanation for hunting. I cannot even explain why I hunt. For me, as for most hunters, there are many reasons—a few obvious, others not so obvious.

This overview of my twenty-five years' experience in Alaska attempts to show how important wildlife and the outdoors are to individuals. You will read of trappers, hunters, guides, wildlife photographers, and biologists. If you are challenged to think more about our unique wild heritage, then the book has been a success. But some of what you read will not be pleasing. I make no apologies: I strove for honesty.

He prayeth well, who loveth well
Both man and bird and beast.

Samuel Taylor Coleridge (1772–1834)
Rime of the Ancient Mariner

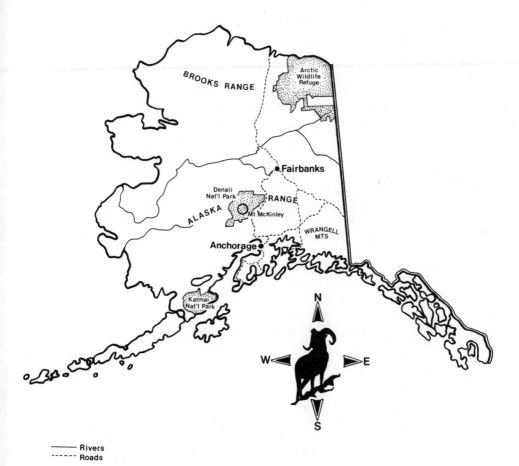

BROOKS RANGE

Arctic
Wildlife
Refuge

•Fairbanks

Denali
Nat'l Park

ALASKA   RANGE

Mt McKinley

WRANGELL
MTS

Anchorage•

Katmai
Nat'l Park

N

W   E

S

——— Rivers
------- Roads

ONE

GRIZZLIES
The Real Bear

I

Far across Prince William Sound, dawn's quicksilver sky backlighted the sawtoothed Chugach Mountains. Bob and I walked down from the cabin to the beach. After a night in the musty cabin, I could almost taste the forest, sea, and salt.

We took a long look at the glowing sky, the flocks of gulls swirling above their sea stack rookeries, and the tendrils of mists lazing above the mudflats. Then we turned and headed up the beach on the seven-mile trek to the head of the bay. Some of the world's largest brown bears lived where this island's forested mountains sloped down to the sea; Bob wanted one.

The low tide at five A.M. had exposed ten square miles of tidal flats. Although burdened with fifty-pound packs, we found easy walking on the exposed mud. In places untouched by high water the ground was hard and cracked like a desert wash. Elsewhere we slogged along over clinging gumbo. In two places we detoured around quagmires. Unwary men and animals have bogged down in such places and drowned in the returning tide.

Tracks and the curled droppings of birds laced the seashell-littered mud. Everywhere the tiny three-toed tracks of dunlins crossed the big webbed prints of dusky Canada geese. Where alders and willows bordered the flats, the tracks of Sitka deer looped into the open.

In the first of the many deep sloughs that segmented the flats, we spooked a flock of mallards. In their wake a few goldeneyes and mergansers ran flapping up the slough in clumsy escape. Higher, skeins of ducks and cranes passed by, heading north to their nesting grounds.

In silence we shared the dawn delights. During the long dark winter there had been only snow and silence; now each slough, each patch of mud, each brushline held evidence of life. Later in the day, even the first mosquito bite of summer would be welcomed, a thing to talk of and be thankful for. Winter was over.

Although the sloughs were only twenty or thirty feet wide, each was at least six feet deep. Travel was tiring. We walked down each cutbank, waded the watercourse, then climbed the opposite side, each step releasing the pungent smell of sulphur. More than once we slipped on the slimy mud. Because of these sloughs, only at low tide could the flats be crossed. At other times the only route to the head of the bay is a long and torturous inland journey through brush and forest shintangle.

Two miles from base camp, we crossed the trail of a brown bear, its pawprints etched into the mud. The tracks looked fresh. Under my pack-straps, I shrugged my shoulders, reveling in the amber light of the rising sun and its growing warmth. Although I often curse the rain, wind, and cold of the coast, I've never visited a more magical place than where these forested mountains slope into the sea. Here I've seen a female brown bear nurse her new cubs, killer whales breach and splash into the sea, eagles swoop to catch fish, and cranes dance in mating ritual. Once I saw a brown bear emerge from the timber with one side of its face white with porcupine quills.

Two hours of hard walking brought us to the end of the mudflats and the beginning of the snow-dotted sedge fields. Here we crossed the snow-packed sloughs with ease.

In another hour or so we left the sedge fields behind and entered the forest. My companion had never been in a coastal rain forest before and he remarked on the thick moss carpet and long skeins of lichen growing on the trees. He also wanted to know who had built the trails.

"Bears."

The trail and forest sparkled with tiny waterholes, excavations about six inches deep and five inches across where bears had rooted skunk cabbage after the autumn salmon runs. I showed Bob the depressions in the trail where generations of bears had stepped in one another's tracks.

We followed the trail for a mile or so before leaving it to turn east toward a range of low hills. The forest skirted open fields dotted with potholes, some crowded with pintails and teal.

I led the way straight across country, checking position by a tall peak visible above the timber. In the low hills we made camp in the old familiar clearing where a cache of extra gear hung in a tree. From this spike camp we'd be able to hunt the mountains as well as the flats. In two hours we had the tent pitched beneath a sheltering tree.

After a late lunch of pilot bread, cheese, sausage, and gorp, we loaded our daypacks and hiked toward the river and mountains beyond. Bear trails strewn with the jaws and bones of last year's salmon feast crisscrossed the heavy alder thickets crowding the riverbanks. On the far bank we found a tree scratched clean of bark up to a height of nine feet, with woolly bear hair clinging to the oozing sap. Blowdowns bore unmistakable claw marks where bears had clambered over. Next to several large trees we found daybeds hollowed out of the moss and duff.

The mountains rose just beyond the river, and soon after crossing it we started up. Hip boots aren't made for climbing and we worked to keep our footing on the steep pitch—the kind of work expected on a goat hunt. Where we could, we used the brush and tree limbs to pull ourselves upward, carefully avoiding the spiny devil's club.

Less than five hundred feet above the river the slope moderated, the dense timber giving way to an alpland dotted with pockets of wind-twisted spruce and mountain hemlock. Here the going was easy as we walked on the hard crust of a still thick snow cover. After wandering the open benches, we reached the summit of one of the lower peaks in early evening.

From our vantage point we could look north to the high peaks surrounding the sound, east and south over the lowlands to the Gulf of Alaska, and west to the island's summit escarpment. Some of the steeper slopes around us were snowless, but mostly the alpland was winterscape.

We glassed the south-facing slopes, the bears' ancestral denning grounds, well into evening. Despite the clear skies, the wind still cut like winter and we wore everything we had. I looked not only for bears, but for tracks and den sites as well. Even three miles away, tracks the size of dinner plates would show up in the right light.

Bob had never seen a brown bear before, and in new country it takes some experience to judge distance and size. All the shapes he pointed out were rocks, some of them bigger than houses. He did spot two deer walking across a snow-covered slope, but he thought they were a mile away instead of the actual half-mile: Sitka deer are smaller than the mule deer he was familiar with.

Late that day we hiked back to camp after seeing only a handful of deer and no bears or their tracks.

The lack of bear sign was bothersome. It was mid-May and with all the snow in the high country, few bears would yet be active. Although weather could alter the pattern, I'd learned that large males emerge from denning first, followed by single females and females with older cubs, then—up to a month later—females with newborn cubs. Bob's chances would improve with time.

The next morning we awoke to a hard rain, unaware that the sun would not shine again for six days. In the next week we hunted the lowlands, beaches, and shores, seeing no bears and only a few tracks. In the face of the cold and constant rain, it was hard to remain cheerful and optimistic. I put on a good front. Many hunters come to Alaska with such high expectations that when they face the reality of not finding a bear behind every bush, they easily become downcast. Bob was no different. He wasn't rich and had saved a long time for his life's dream trip. After days of rain and fruitless searching, he was depressed.

On the ninth day the rain stopped and we saw our first bear.

A few hours before dark we headed for a lake about a mile from camp. I led the way through heavy timber and brush, aware of the sounds we made. Other than the sound of human voices, the slap of limbs against hip boots or raingear is the most unnatural sound in the woods.

We worked our way into the blowdowns along the lake and found a vantage point to glass the shoreline. We saw two black-and-white mergansers noisily fighting over a drab hen, and a goldeneye displaying for its mate. On the far side of the lake, in front of an abandoned beaver house rooted open by bears, four geese bobbed near two trumpeter swans.

The far bank was lush with fresh grass, an encouraging sign, so we decided to keep watch until dark. Under the bright afternoon sun, the antics of the mating waterfowl kept us entertained. For the first time in days, Bob looked relaxed.

At dusk the swans' nervous honking drew my attention to the far end of the lake. There, a female (I prefer not to use the common terms *sow* and *boar* because of their primary association with swine) and what looked to be her two-year-old cub cropped the new grass. Under his breath Bob whistled at their size, though they were both, at least to me, relatively small bears.

We watched as long as we could before sneaking away in the dark, leaving the bears undisturbed.

The clear weather held and over the next two days we hunted the river flats in the morning and the highlands in the afternoon. Up high each day, through binoculars and aided by the slanting sun, we picked out new bear trails crossing distant snow patches. Below an outcropping on the side of the island's highest peak we located a den in the snow, many trails leading to and fro.

At the first hint of darkness on the eleventh day, with a stillness creeping through the forest, we settled into stands overlooking the river.

Just at sundown the wind died down. Behind me lichen-draped spruce towered into the air, their crowns so thick that only a few devil's club, berry bushes, and skunk cabbage grew on the forest floor. A Stellar jay flitted through the timber to alight on a limb. I sat glassing the head of the bay. A

few yards away Bob sat facing the flats. We were watching the forest edge to
the west and northwest where a few days before we'd found the tracks and
droppings of a lone bear. Apparently it had fed there often and we'd
decided then that each early morning and late evening until the end of the
hunt we'd watch for it.

I had no way of knowing whether the wait would be fruitful but I've
hunted as many as fourteen straight days—not eight-hour days but nine-
teen-hour days—waiting for a bear to move into the open. When skulking
in the living forest in the gray twilight of dawn or evening, waiting for a
bear to emerge from the timber, I feel most like the primal hunter.

I lifted my glasses and studied the far tree line. In the preceding days I'd
looked there so often that I knew every bush by heart. Every bush, that is,
but the one by the broken spruce at the head of the bay. The one . . .

Wait! That's no bush. That's a bear! A big one.

Where just minutes before there had been nothing, now a bear stood
sniffing at the night air.

I gave the signal, the low hoot of an owl. I kept my eyes on the bear,
knowing Bob would hurry over. It was imperative to watch the bear's every
move, judge its every reaction, and try to predict its intentions. A big bear is
both old and wise and, knowing the dangers, will come into the open only
at night, then with caution. I chastised myself for being so excited. It
seemed so unprofessional. This was no first bear. No first hunt. But again, I
knew what could happen.

Bob raised his binoculars and gasped. This bear, now feeding into the
open, was much bigger then the ones we'd seen before. While shucking our
windbreakers, coats, and excess gear, I whispered a plan. We'd backtrack a
short distance, then run across the flats to the far side and make the stalk
along the timber's edge.

We made the run in a crouch and reached the timber out of breath.
My one big concern evaporated: the faint breeze blew from the bear to us.
We could make the stalk.

Bears see better than is commonly believed, and we used every bit of
cover as we hurried up the bay. This kind of hunt is always a gamble, and
we couldn't waste time. We had no way of knowing how long the bear
would be in the open. All too soon it could be in the timber again.

Both wind and cover favored us, but many things could spoil our stalk.
We'd have to get close quickly. If it grew too dark, or if the bear fed too
close to the timber, we could not shoot. The bear had to be well into the

open to allow a backup shot. Too close to the timber and a shot would be risky: the wounded bear could get away.

Three hundred yards from where we'd last seen the bear we stopped to glass but saw nothing. It looked as if he had gone back into the timber.

A minute later I raised my binoculars in time to see the bear climbing the riverbank two hundred yards away. While crossing the river he'd been out of sight below the cutbank. Well into the open, he again stopped to crop the spring grass.

Here was our opportunity. We could use the brush along the river to sneak within one hundred yards. There'd be time, too, if need be, for a second or perhaps even a third backup shot.

Careful not to brush against limbs or step on fallen branches, we weaved through the scattered alder to the river and crossed below its confluence with a feeder stream. On the other side I motioned for Bob to chamber a round in his .375. I did the same, then took some shells from my belt pouch and put them into my right pants pocket.

Side by side we crawled over the bank and took prone shooting positions. The bear fed about a hundred twenty-five yards away. *"Wait until the bear turns broadside,"* I whispered to Bob, *"then shoot through the shoulders, and break him down. A lung-shot bear has the strength to run into the brush. Don't squeeze the trigger unless you are sure."*

Now our fate was solely in Bob's hands. He was an experienced hunter, but this was his first bear and anything could happen. Hunters read and tell too damn many bearchew stories. *Any* bear, *any* circumstance, puts them on edge.

Through the rifle scope I got a good look at the bear quartering away from us. It looked to be a male—big, blocky, powerful, a veteran of many mating battles. Even in the dimming light I could see scars along his side and flanks. He looked to weigh around eight hundred pounds, but in the fall, after fattening on salmon and berries, he might go over a thousand.

The bear turned broadside. Bob fired, his .375 spitting flame a foot long. I heard the WHUMP! of the bullet and saw the bear stagger but in a breath it was up and running back the way it had come.

"Shoot! Shoot again!" I shouted. The sharp crack of the big rifle answered but the bear kept going. I couldn't wait any longer. Already the bear was to the alders on the river's edge. I'd given Bob two shots. I had to prevent the wounded bear's escape. I swung the open bead past the bear's nose and squeezed the trigger. The .375 Whitworth hammered me and in the instant I worked the bolt I knew that I had missed. The bear went over the cutbank. In the long moment he was out of sight I hoped he'd gone down, but instead he came up the opposite bank in an all-out rush for the timber. He was angling away and too far for open sights. Bob took one more shot before the bear was gone.

In the sudden silence I stood staring at the open flats. Seconds ago the bear had been there, now nothing. Instead of a dead bear to skin we had a wounded one to follow. I waved Bob silent and together we walked to where the bear had been.

I paced off the distance as I walked—one hundred forty yards. It was a little far but not too far. We had broken the first rule of bear hunting: make the first shot count. I found the muddy tracks and the torn sod where the bear had wheeled to run. Backtracking to the alders, I found a tree limb my bullet had clipped. I waded the river and followed the bear's tracks across the wet rocks and up the bank. My finger on the trigger, safety off, expecting the unexpected, I tracked the bear to the edge of the timber. I took off my hat and put it down where the trail entered the brush.

We backed away from the timber to talk things over. There was no blood. Not a drop. Bob said that he doubted that he could've missed completely. I knew he hadn't. I'd heard and seen the bear react. We retraced our steps, checking for blood or patches of hair. Although it was getting darker all the time, we had enough light to see that there was no blood. Already it was too dark to track the bear into the forest.

We walked back to where I'd left my hat. I picked it up and marked the spot by tying a piece of cloth to an overhanging branch. While Bob waited in the open, I stepped into the forest tangle twenty yards from the marker. Before dark I wanted all the information I could get.

Under the spruce canopy it was darker and every bush, stump, and blowdown looked like a bear, or at least, like one could be hiding there. I moved away from the brush and stood with my back to a giant spruce. The timber, rubble, and underbrush favored the bear. A charge here, now, would be point-blank.

In the next fifteen minutes I saw and heard nothing, not even a bird call. In darkness I rejoined my hunter and told him the news. We started for camp at a fast walk.

That night I slept little. I kept thinking of the bear. This was only the second time that a wounded bear had gotten away from me. I didn't like it. I never wanted to see an animal suffer, or to waste one.

Next morning we were up at five. The sky was clear and the wind calm. It was just what we needed. Even a light rain would've washed away the sign. We bolted down breakfast before hurrying off.

Back at the head of the bay we again tracked the bear. Even in broad daylight we could not find a single drop of blood.

We entered the timber together, moving slowly, looking in all directions. The spongy moss had soaked up all tracks and at once we lost the trail. In ever-widening circles we hunted for tracks, blood, or other clues. For at least an hour we searched the area by the marker and found nothing.

Although it seemed relatively unlikely that an injured bear would climb such a steep hillside, I made a wide loop upward to study the new terrain. Nothing. I rejoined Bob in the open. His disappointment was obvious. He told me to give up, the bear was gone. He said since there was no blood it seemed probable that the bear wasn't badly hurt. But we couldn't give up. The vitality of even a wounded bear can be phenomenal, and we had to keep looking.

We made another loop, this time climbing higher than before, searching the ground with care. Then we went over the old terrain again. Even healthy bears leave tracks. *Somewhere* in the sphagnum carpet there had to be a track or other sign. Bob sat down and shook his head. He said he was disgusted with his shooting, and if he didn't find this one, he would never hunt another bear.

Again leaving Bob behind, I climbed a quarter-mile up the hill into the thickest timber. Looking right and left, I moved like *I* expected to be shot at. In the thick moss below the steepest slope I found the front paw print of a large bear.

I searched downhill and found nothing, but uphill from the track, I found another track, then another. A few feet farther I found one drop of blood on a leaf. Just one. A few yards farther, two drops. Then a few feet more, a bright splash. Then more. And more.

Over half a mile from where the bear had been shot I had found the first drop of blood. The trail turned up an almost perpendicular slope. There I could no longer follow the track while watching ahead for the bear. I took off my shirt and tied it around a tree and headed back to get Bob. The incline led back to a point directly above where the bear had entered the woods, a place we'd searched twice.

Bob sat on a blowdown at the edge of the flats but stood as I walked up. I could read the dismay in his eyes. I reached into my pocket and pulled out a leaf smeared with blood. He shed his pack, and at a trot we started back.

I reclaimed my shirt and picked up the trail. While I tracked, Bob followed a few feet behind, watching upslope for the bear that could be hiding behind any of the big spruce or blowdowns.

Uprooted moss and overturned stones marked the bear's trail. It was a slow, intense process: study the ground, search ahead, climb a few feet. Study the ground, search ahead, climb a few feet. If the bear were to charge straight downhill, we'd never stop it.

A few hundred feet up the hill we came to a bad place. Just above us was a bench, a place for the bear to rest or wait in ambush. If we kept climbing and the bear was there, we would not know it until eyeball to eyeball. After talking things over and warning Bob to be ready, I left the blood trail and made a wide swing to the north. In a few minutes I was level with the bench and could see that the bear wasn't there. But earlier, it had been. Blood-soaked moss marked where the bear, in perfect defilade, had waited, facing his back trail.

A few feet above the bench we lost the trail. What had been obvious before was now imperceptible. Time and again we circled, trying to pick up the track. No blood, no broken branches, no torn moss. Finally I found one overturned rock about the size of a golf ball and a little farther on, one tiny drop of blood. Then a broken twig and some claws marks on a log. In an hour we were back on track but climbing at a slower pace.

At one point, while clinging with hands and feet to the hillside, I knew why some hunters *never* follow up wounded bears. The risk is too high. But there's an ethic involved, a certain responsibility that comes with shooting a bear. Personal concerns come second, and if for no other reason than to stop an animal's suffering, or to ensure there's no waste, every wounded bear—*any* animal, for that matter—must be trailed until the denouement.

Near the summit of the ridge, sixteen hundred feet from the river, we found blood stains behind a dead snag. Here again we lost the trail. For an hour we searched the immediate area, neither of us wanting our first glimpse of the bear to be a blurring charge from close range. In silence, we approached each possible hiding place with tense fingers on triggers.

Bob took a direct line away from the bed and went south; I went north. When I was two hundred yards away, I heard Bob hoot like an owl. I hurried to where he stood. Behind a large spruce was another blood-soaked bed, an obvious trail leading away. Ten yards farther was another bed. Five more yards then still another. Here the trail turned straight downhill. Where earlier we'd tracked the bear by finding a drop of blood, or crushed leaf, or an overturned stone, we now followed a trail anyone could've followed.

A hundred yards downhill we came to an alder thicket, the big limbs broken and pushed aside. Hunkering down, I looked underneath the canopy. A dark form filled an opening fifteen yards away. I drew back and leveled my rifle, but there was no movement. I waited, and in the wait knew the bear was dead.

I looked at my watch. It was 1:30. We'd been tracking since 6:30. Over seven hours of high tension. It was enough.

The thought of packing the one hundred and twenty-five pounds of hide back to the cabin didn't bother me. The burden seemed only right. While skinning the bear we found bullet fragments under the ribs. Only one bullet, the first, had struck the bear. It had torn through the bottom of both lungs and fragmented beneath the diaphragm. By the extent of the wound it seemed likely that the bear probably died within the hour of being shot, twelve hundred feet above and almost one and a half miles from the tidal flats.

II

"Goin' huntin', eh?" the old fisherman asked of the young man passing by.
"Yep. Going after a bear."
"Shoot fifty," said the fisherman, picking up the net he mended.
"Excuse me?"
"Shoot fifty. Kill 'em all. Get rid of 'em. They ain't safe. They ain't no good. Besides, they eat fish."

Cordova boat harbor, 1986

Twenty years ago, despite stable bear populations, sourdough pundits predicted that the big bears would soon become relics. Many of these old-timers remembered a time in the not-so-distant past when bears were shot as vermin in a campaign to rid the country of the "bruin menace." The expanding human population pressure had many Alaskans concerned. Today, confounding the seers, bears have *increased* until they are more numerous than at any time since the 1930s.

Biologists attribute the increase to sound research and management programs. Since statehood several positive changes have been made in the hunting laws: it is now illegal to hunt the same day as airborne, in effect making it unlawful to spot a bear, then land nearby and shoot it; cubs, as well as females with cubs, are protected; seasons are segmented into spring and fall and set so that little hunting occurs when bears are concentrated along salmon streams; hunters are allowed only one bear every four years; nonresidents must be accompanied by a registered guide; and in some areas, such as the Kodiak National Wildlife Refuge, hunting is by permit only. Also with statehood, federal wolf-poisoning programs came to an end allowing both wolves and bears, as well as all meateaters, to increase.

Nevertheless, in some areas bear populations are lower than in previous years. Habitat destruction and bear-human conflict are prime reasons for the decline.

Contrary to popular myth, not all of Alaska is prime wildlife habitat. Alaskan grizzlies are robust and healthy, sometimes traveling many miles in a single day. In some areas bears need vast tracts of land to eke out survival. For the most part, the wildlands still belong to them but their country is shrinking. The same pressures that resulted in their extirpation in much of the Lower Forty-Eight are developing here. In the early nineteenth century northern California, an area much smaller than Alaska, supported ten thousand grizzlies. A hundred years later there were none. Once there were thought to be one hundred thousand grizzlies roaming the West. Now there are fewer than nine hundred.

Perhaps thirty-five thousand browns and grizzlies live in Alaska, utilizing habitat as diverse as the dense rain forests of Alaska's panhandle and the North Slope barrens. Although hunting records books identify two distinct species, coastal brown bears and interior grizzlies with arbitrarily designated ranges, both names refer to the same species. Quality habitat (parts of Admiralty and Kodiak islands) supports one bear per square mile; poor habitat (the North Slope), one bear per three hundred square miles. In comparison, the highest known grizzly densities in the contiguous United States occur in Glacier National Park, with one bear per eight square miles. Yellowstone's resource managers hope to restore the population to a high of one bear per twenty-eight square miles. In unique feeding situations Alaskan bears congregate in large numbers. At McNeil River State Game Sanctuary, one biologist estimated that more than one hundred bears were coming to the falls to catch salmon. Once, in the quarter-mile of river below the falls, he saw a congregation of sixty.

Nowhere are bears reproductively prolific. In the high Arctic, females may not successfully breed until eight or nine years of age. Bears within Fish and Game researcher Sterling Miller's study area near the Susitna River breed at age five; most have their first litters at age six, the earliest recorded in Alaska. Female bears with cubs do not breed again until the cubs go off on their own, usually a minimum of two years after birth but sometimes as much as five years. Since few bears in the wild live longer than twenty-five years, the reproductive potential for each female is low. A high death rate among females carries the potential for population catastrophe.

Alaska's bears now may roam over habitat only slightly altered by humans, but times *are* changing. Demographers predict that at current rates Alaska's human population in the next twenty years will double to more than one million. Wildlands are being cleared for farms and urban centers. In just a few short years the land around Anchorage and in the Matanuska Valley, as well as in the Tanana Valley around Fairbanks, has become urbanized and developed. Stores and homes cover the land once used by moose, bear, and waterfowl. The raw wounds of the earth bleed beneath concrete, steel, and tarmac scabs.

At Point MacKenzie thousands of forested acres have been cleared for dairy farms, another state-subsidized project. Mouthing fatuous statements, politicians push for accelerated agricultural development, saying it is one of the state's top priorities. If indeed this were a public priority, the state would not allow the prime agricultural land in the Matanuska and Tanana valleys to be turned into housing tracts and shopping malls. The land cleared across from Anchorage is also for expansion, when one day a bridge spans Knik Arm. Simply because it will become too valuable for farming, the cleared land will vanish as fast as the wildlife before it.

Forty-four million acres of land is passing into private ownership under the terms of the 1971 Alaska Native Claims Settlement Act. Already, heavy logging on Native lands on Admiralty Island has brought habitat destruction, direct killing of bears by logging crews, and displacement by disturbance. Similar scenes have unfolded on Afognak Island, as well as other parts of Southeast Alaska. Proposed logging around Prince William Sound, and elsewhere, will only exacerbate the situation. Giant hydroelectric projects are in planning; mineral and oil exploration continues. The classic confrontation on Kodiak between stockmen and bears pits man's self-interest and economics against wildlife. These are the same conflicts that led to the elimination of grizzlies from much of their southern range.

Unfortunately, the conservation of Alaska's natural resources is entangled in the political-legal morass of well-intentioned national legislation. The Alaska Native Claims Settlement Act of 1971 (ANCSA), the Marine Mammal Protection Act of 1972, and the Alaska National Interest Lands Conservation Act (ANILCA) of 1980, have resulted in complex legalities that bode ill for Alaska's people and wildlife. ANILCA, for example, mandates huge annual cuts of timber in the Tongass National Forest *regardless* of market conditions or environmental impacts. This act also mandated "subsistence preference" for rural hunters, which makes it virtually impossible in some instances to enforce conservative regulations. Under the terms of the Marine Mammal Protection Act, Alaska Natives can hunt polar bears without regard to sex or age, season or bag limit. Cubs, as well as females with cubs, once protected by Alaska law, now may be hunted by Natives at any time of the year.

Long shadows creep over the future of Alaska's great bears.

"The moose must've been hit by a car and died after running into the brush. Almost one whole day I sat watching the brown bear feeding on the carcass just forty yards from the road. It was a bigger thrill than anything I ever had hunting. Then some guy stopped and, right while I was parked there, tried to shoot the bear. And the season wasn't even open. Can't people appreciate them for what they are? Without shooting everything?"

—Hunter, Cooper Landing, 1985

III

In the long night and subzero temperatures of Brooks Range winter, a howling wind shrieks down the slopes of Crag Peak. Near the base of the mountain, in a den beneath the insulating snow, a female grizzly stirs from hibernation to give birth to three hairless cubs, each weighing less than a pound. After licking them clean and eating the afterbirths, she snuggles the cubs close to her warm chest and drifts back to sleep. Instinctively, they begin to suckle.

Back in October, the bear, waddling fat from gorging on a bumper crop of blueberries, had sought this den for her winter's rest. Her last few days above ground had been spent napping at the mouth of her den, or idling close by. Protected by her thick fur and heavy fat layer, she seemed

heedless of the cold and snow that had already fallen. As the days short-
ened, diminishing sunlight triggered an increase of melatonin within her
brain that brought on her lethargy and then hibernation. In these harsh
arctic mountains, she, like most of her kind, will spend almost six and a half
months in her den.

The previous June, during the peak of breeding season, she had come
into estrus at age eight for the first time in her life. In her restless spring
wanderings she had traveled to the Wild River on the edge of her usual
range and, after an often violent courting, was bred by a five hundred–
pound male that soon left to follow the scent trail of another female. The
fertilized egg, in a phenomenon scientists call delayed implantation, stayed
dormant until denning time, when it attached to the uterine wall and began
normal gestation.

In May, when she emerges from the den with her cubs, each then
weighing about twelve pounds, she will be an aggressive, protective mother.
Using her superb sense of smell, she will attempt to lead her cubs to food
and keep them safe. They will learn to fear the scent of other bears and
follow their mother as she leads them from danger. She knows that mature
males will try to kill and eat her cubs, and she will defend them fiercely. In
fact, the mother-young bond in bears is so powerful that not infrequently
females will adopt orphan cubs as their own. For three years, perhaps even
four or five, the cubs will stay with their mother, sharing her wisdom as
well as her den, until one spring she again comes into heat and drives them
away, the bond forever broken.

The spring and summer pattern will follow the dictates of hunger. Just
after leaving the den, the female will be thin, over the winter having lost
almost one third of her autumn body weight. In this critical time she will
lead her cubs in search of leftover berries, winter kills, or perhaps, if lucky, a
calf moose. As summer progresses, she and her cubs will live easy and fatten
on greens, roots, insects, rodents, carrion, and the very few large mammals
she may bring down. On the arctic slope some bears feed on char, and
along the coast they gorge on salmon, but in this bear's home range there
are no fish, and the ripening of the berries becomes an important event.
Unlike birds, which pick individual berries from a stem, she will grasp an
entire blueberry branch in her paws and with her mouth strip it of fruit,
leaves, bugs, everything.

In late autumn, after the insect plague has ended with the chill immi-
nence of winter, if the berry crop has been good, she will once again enter

the den in top condition. If the berries have failed because of too much or too little rain, or too hot or too cold weather, she may die in winter or in early spring. In times of famine, some females do not bear young; others are unable to care for their cubs. For them, a failed berry crop can be a disaster.

But it is still winter, and the female moans softly in her sleep as the cubs pull and tug at her nipples, the rich milk flowing sweet and good. Over the thick snow dome of her den, the wind tears at the crusted snow. High overhead, handful upon handful of gems wink in the night, while somewhere nearby a wolf's howl harkens to spring.

IV

There's a story hard for me to tell. It's of a monumental error in judgment as well as a display of naïveté. Stupidity.

Long before I could afford a camera, I was interested in wildlife photography. In 1966 I bought my first 35mm camera and telephoto lens, a $40 400mm with all the clarity of a focusable pop bottle. Not long afterward a Fairbanks cinematographer showed me a grizzly film he'd shot in McKinley Park, all superb footage with one spellbinding sequence of a prime grizzly by a sparkling stream. This was a shot of just the bear's head as it munched the grass and wildflowers. Once, the bear looked up and straight into the camera. That one glance spoke volumes.

It was all very impressive, but the footage taken by his son that showed the cinematographer filming not thirty feet from the grizzly was *stunning*. Everything I had heard, read, or imagined, labeled this as insanity. Under questioning, our host stated in emphatic terms that park bears were harmless. All that stuff about danger was hype. "Just walk right up and take their picture," he said, "that is, if they don't run away."

At first I was unconvinced. Yet, at the same time, I did not *know*. How *did* those guys get those pictures I saw in the magazines?

The following July, my partner, a young cinematographer, and I teamed up in McKinley Park for a week of photography. In stark contrast to today, there were few people in the park, and wildlife was plentiful. Under cloudless skies, we made stills and movies of Dall sheep, moose, caribou, and once, a wolf, but what we really wanted were bear pictures. My partner was eager to duplicate sequences in the film we'd seen. Over the course of the week we stalked two lone bears, but as predicted, both ran off.

Late one sun-splashed day in a swale above the Toklat River, we found a female with two cubs grazing on lush summer grass. It looked like the ideal place for photography, and the family group was an appealing subject. We left the road and made our approach. I went east to use a willow and alder thicket as cover, while my companion approached the bears in the open from the west.

When I finally got my tripod set up behind a brushline less than seventy-five yards from the bears, my companion already was filming them from the opposite side of the swale. The bears seemed to ignore us. While making the stalk I'd had misgivings, but at this point they seemed groundless.

I took one picture, advanced the film, then moved two steps closer. After repositioning my tripod I looked up. One of the cubs was standing on its hindlegs, looking at me. Just as I released the shutter a second time I felt a gust of wind at my back. Both cubs started to mill around. The female looked at her cubs, then looked at me. All at once I felt extremely vulnerable and exposed. She hesitated but a moment, then brushing aside a cub, charged. I knew she wasn't going to stop.

Grabbing my camera, I ducked low behind the brushline and ran. I wanted to get to the gully and out of sight. When the bear saw me again, I wanted to be far enough away so that she'd see that I meant her cubs no harm.

In four of five strides I was in the gully and running downhill. Halfway down I looked over my shoulder just as the bear charged over the top. I panicked into full flight. Ten yards downhill I gained control and turned to face her. No way was I going to be pulled down from behind. I braced myself, my tripod gripped like a rifle and bayonet.

She covered the intervening ground in a flash. I lunged at her with all my strength, jabbing the camera toward her face. It seemed I couldn't miss, but with stunning agility the bear swerved away and I flailed thin air. She stopped not five yards from me. I thrust at her again, but again missed as she jumped away. As swiftly as she had charged, she now raced off toward her cubs waiting at the top of the gully. With only brief backward glances the bears went over the crest and were gone.

For a long moment, I stood motionless in the gully, too stupid to be scared. Until the very last second, I'd done everything wrong that a person can do around bears and escaped without a scratch. I was never out of her sight, for example, and running away had only encouraged assault. Though unaware of it at the time, I was suffering from near-terminal macho. I saw this as another adventure. Even standing next to me—literally arm's length—the bear looked small, standing less than waist high. I convinced myself that when I lunged the second time, I knew by the look in her eyes that I had won the upper hand.

When I got back to the road, a few people had gathered near our vehicle. One man said that he had never seen a more courageous act. "You're a fool," snapped another. (He was correct.)

"Where's the water jug?" I said.

In hindsight I'm amazed by—and thankful for—the close escape. Even back then, despite the anesthesia of youth, reality didn't take long to sink in. About a month later I awoke yelling in the night. In a vivid dream I had remembered two things I'd blocked out. Every time the bear's front paws struck the ground, her jaws snapped closed with a loud pop. What haunted me more, then as now, was the clear picture of her paws clearing the ground, those long white claws clicking together, scything the air like ten giant razors.

V

All the trouble I've ever had with bears has been of my own doing. I've never had to shoot a brown-grizzly in self-defense, but once I killed a black bear that came sniffing around the small tent where I was sleeping. I awoke to see a bear peering in through the mosquito netting, its face less than *thirty inches* from mine. He bolted when I sat up, but when he came back, I shot him. The fault was mine. Because of rain the night before, instead of cooking well away from the tent, I had prepared dinner inside and left some food on the stove—a sure invitation for trouble.

Since my initial years of blundering about the country, I've had little trouble with bears. By learning their ways, where they live, what they eat, and how they seem to view the world, I've managed to avoid problems. I rue the youthful ignorance that resulted in the killing of that black bear.

Simple ignorance—or is it human arrogance that disdains the "lesser" creatures?—brings about many problems. Where bear-human conflicts arise, no matter the fault, the solution is often gunfire. Once several years ago I walked into the covered ramp above Cordova's small boat harbor and saw a hand-lettered sign with the skinned front paws of a black bear nailed to it. "He stole from my boat," the sign read, "so I cut off his hands."

There's just no way to know how many bear-human encounters occur each year in Alaska but with all the hikers, climbers, berry pickers, campers, hunters, and fishermen who go afield each year, it says something about bears that so few people get hurt. Unless they are surprised or their critical distance—which varies from one animal and circumstance to another—is violated, the bears' superb senses keep them out of trouble. They avoid contact whenever possible.

Alaska's bears are known by many names: *grizzly . . . griz . . . brownie . . . Kodiak . . . silvertip.* Interior Athabascans have several words for brown-grizzly bears. One translates as "bad animal." Another means "those who are in the mountains," and reflecting the people's attitude towards bears, one means "keep out of its way."

Around the turn of the century, scientists described about ninety subspecies of brown and grizzly bears in North America, the differences based on variations in size, hair color, skull shape, as well as other variables. Now they recognize just one highly variable species of brown-grizzly bear, *Ursus arctos.*

Both black bears and brown-grizzly bears can be encountered anywhere in Alaska, even inside the Fairbanks, Anchorage, and Juneau city limits. Black bears, *Ursus americanus,* are the more abundant and widespread of North American bears and are found throughout all forested areas of Alaska as well as parts of the lower forty-eight states, Canada, and Mexico.

Both brown-grizzlies and black bears have color vision, long memory retention, and the ability to discriminate form, size, and shape of an object—important survival and food-gathering tools.

Despite the descriptive names, bears can not be identified solely by color. Black bears vary from the rare white phase, found in British Columbia, through brown and cinnamon to the blue, or glacier phase, localized to the Yakutat region. Brown-grizzlies can be black to blond and all the shades between.

In some circumstances, especially with immature or cub bears, field identification can be difficult. A black bear has a brown muzzle, a straight facial profile, long ears, short curving claws, and no shoulder hump. Brown-grizzlies have a curving facial profile, shorter ears, long straight claws, and a prominent shoulder hump. They are also much bigger than black bears: most males weigh four hundred to nine hundred pounds, and females, half that. A few individuals, always males, reach fourteen hundred pounds. The record for the wild is a coastal male that weighed in at 1,656 pounds. Although few Alaskan black bears go over four hundred pounds, a lot less than the scale-busters found near dumps and orchards in the eastern United States, size alone does not provide accurate identification because, to the untrained eye, especially at close range, every bear looks big. If I'm ever in doubt, say at night or in thick brush, I act as if facing a brown-grizzly.

Each year one or two people in Alaska are bitten by black and brown-grizzly bears, and every six or eight years someone is killed. The attacks always make headlines, but if the same fatalities were due to disease or common accidents, they wouldn't even warrant reportorial comment.

Although it is dangerous to make simple statements about animal behavior, it is a common perception in Alaska that coastal bears, because of their abundant food sources, salmon and berries, display a remarkable tolerance toward humans, unlike their irascible kin in interior Alaska that, at times, know famine. Kodiak Island, for example, has one of the highest densities of bears in Alaska but no record of fatalities in fifty or sixty years, and only five or six injuries in the last ten years. Stories of vengeful monarchs killing humans on Kodiak are fiction.

Within recent memory, in sharp contrast to popular belief, only two people—a photographer at Cold Bay and a camper in Glacier Bay—have been killed by brown bears. Bears *are* dangerous but unprovoked attacks are rare. There is always a reason. The two major ways humans come into conflict with bears are surprise close-range encounters and when bears obtain food from people.

Except during the breeding season, bears have two very simple motivations—food and self-protection. A study in Denali Park concluded that one grizzly spent over eighty percent of its waking moments either feeding or searching for food. It should be obvious that bears will investigate any potential source of food, most vigorously where natural forage is lacking or difficult to obtain. Trouble brews when a bear follows its nose to the food smells emanating from a human habitation.

Black bears and brown-grizzlies differ in their reaction to danger. Black bears tend to flee more readily than brown-grizzlies. Biologists theorize that different survival strategies developed because of habitat. Since black bears live in forested areas, though they sometimes travel into the alpine, they have evolved an instinct to flee rather than fight. They must be wary, for on occasion, a brown-grizzly attempts to kill and eat a black bear. Because brown-grizzlies usually can not climb trees and are more at home in open country, with strength and ferocity their only protection, they are more apt to fight.

The critical variable in human-bear encounters is distance. *The closer a person is to a bear the more likely trouble will ensue.* Whenever one strange bear encounters another, flight or combat results. Bears seem to view close approach as a hostile or aggressive act. Humans entering their space may be viewed in the same context. So that I don't surprise a bear, I always make noise while hiking. Whenever possible, I walk with the wind at my back, so that my scent will reach the bear before I do, and I avoid hiking in thick brush, where chance encounters are more likely. In the event I do meet a bear unexpectedly, I stand my ground. After a moment, I speak softly to let the bear know that I'm a human and not another bear. Too, I think the tone of my voice can communicate a message, although of course there's no way to prove that. Females accompanied by cubs are especially volatile, perhaps judging any encroachment on their space as a threat to their young. A bear can run thirty to thirty-five miles an hour, about as fast as a whitetail deer, and unless there's a tree, vehicle, or cabin close by, I've learned the hard way that there's no use running.

Given a chance, most bears avoid humans. Sudden encounters between humans and bears usually end with the humans getting a remarkably close look at the south end of a bear heading north in overdrive. If most people would take simple precautions—keep a clean camp, dispose of garbage in a way that doesn't attract bears—they would have nothing to fear. There are exceptions. Wounded or injured bears, bears protecting food, and mating pairs may offer special hazard.

Wildlife photographers and hunters, because the very nature of their activities violates cardinal precepts of living safely with bears, face added risk. All hunters, not just bear hunters, need to exercise extreme caution in the outdoors. Hunters packing in meat, or returning to a kill for the meat, or who have meat hanging in camp, are most in jeopardy. For me the complexion of a hunt changes when meat is in camp. I get edgy and sleep fitfully. I know that a veritable highway of scent is drifting over the forest and tundra, a lure few bears can resist.

Bear hunters take increased risks. Hunting is no child's game. Wounded bears are dangerous and hunters have been attacked. Accepting the risk should be the hunter's responsibility and the bears indemnified from any consequences.

In Denali National Park from 1949 through 1978, ten nonfatal bear attacks were reported. Seven of the ten involved females with cubs, and one other involved two subadult bears. Half the victims were photographers. Without luck, I would have been another statistic.

Black bears also are dangerous. Each year in Alaska they cause most of the property damage and human injury attributable to bears, for several reasons. Statewide, and especially near urban centers, there are more black bears than brown-grizzlies; black bears seem to become accustomed to people more quickly; and humans tend to be more tolerant of black bears near their residences. Finally, and most important, people just don't give black bears due respect. Even a small black bear possesses great strength.

"The most dangerous black bear appears to be one that attacks a person who has been hiking, walking, berry-picking, fishing, or playing during the day in a rural or remote area," writes researcher Stephen Herrero in his book *Bear Attacks.* * "The bear's motivation in this unlikely event most often appears to be predation."

Garbage-habituated brown-grizzlies have accounted for nearly two thirds of all bear-inflicted human injuries inside United States national parks, but Herrero has concluded that garbage and food conditioning have been primary factors in attacks by black bears only infrequently.

"I conclude it is mainly wild black bears found in rural or remote areas—where they have had relatively little association with people—that occasionally try to kill and eat a human being," Herrero writes.

"In fact, the habituated black bear," he says, "seems almost always to be involved only in incidents of minor injuries."

The two human deaths mentioned earlier were apparently the result of predation. At Glacier Bay, a starving bear in poor habitat seems to have killed a person for food. (The victim's camera contained close-ups of a bear, perhaps the killer, and in a macabre twist, Richard Adams's book *Shardik* was found in his destroyed tent.) The facts in the Cold Bay incident, while not as clearcut, seem to point the same way. The victim, a photographer seeking bear pictures, had camped on a well-used bear trail next to a salmon stream; the bear, believed to be in a food-gathering mode, killed and ate the man. At least one authority disagrees with the analysis of both cases and

---

*Herrero, Stephen. *Bear Attacks*. New York: Nick Lyons Books, 1985.

thinks both bears had been used to obtaining human food. In any case, such incidents are rare and outside the realm of normal behavior.

Herrero has identified four circumstances that contribute to bear attacks. Mismanagement of food and garbage is number one. A sudden encounter at close range with a female grizzly and young is next on the list. Human culpability—teasing, chasing, throwing rocks, approaching for photographs—and bears' loss of their natural fear of humans come last.

Despite the illustrations on the covers of outdoor magazines, bears do not attack in a standing position; they charge in a low rush with ears laid back. Most bear attacks are brief, lasting just seconds. The victim suffers extensive wounds, usually to the head and neck.

When a bear does attack a person, it is probably not trying to kill but rather treating the human just as it would another bear guilty of some transgression. An animal powerful enough to kill a mature moose would have no trouble killing a human. I've watched the bears at McNeil River, Katmai, and elsewhere engage in play-fights as well as serious combat, and they always go for one another's muzzle, ears, neck, head, and upper shoulders—the same areas humans suffer injuries. Bears seem to focus on resistance, or at least movement, and as soon as the person stops resisting, the attack ends.

When in bear country, many people carry firearms for self-protection. In Alaska, after other measures have failed, it is legal to kill a bear to defend one's life and property. A written report of the killing must be filed within fifteen days and the hide and skull turned over to the state. In 1987 sixty-four brown-grizzlies were killed in self-defense.

Over the last fifteen years sport hunters have averaged an annual kill of about 934 brown-grizzlies, sixty percent of which were taken by guided nonresidents. An average of 1,151 bears were killed each year from 1984 through 1987; the actual number for 1987 was 1,212. Because an undetermined number of killings go unreported, especially in rural areas, the combined totals cause resource managers concern.

Some experts believe that many bears are killed out of fear and ignorance rather than because of genuine threat to life and property. Veteran guides and hunters spend years in the bush without ever having to kill a bear. They've learned not to attract bears or otherwise create problems.

Firearms are illegal in many of Alaska's national parks. The policy was established to protect wildlife from unnecessary killing. Bears do bluff-charge and not every bluff charge is serious. The National Park Service fears that people would shoot without real need and leave wounded bears wandering about. Each time someone is killed by a bear in a park, debate over the no-firearms rule follows.

Outdoor users who don't condone firearms have varying strategies for preventing bear attacks. Some people tie bells to their packs so that they make noise while hiking, others carry noisemakers, such as firecrackers or compressed air horns like those used on small boats, to scare off bears. Some carry one of the new commercial bear-repellent sprays based on cayenne pepper. Stan Price, who lives on Admiralty Island at the mouth of Pack Creek, a brown bear reserve, carries only a stick with which he thumps troublesome bears. Other people think the scent of mothballs deters trespassing bears and spread them around their camps or tents. A few people refuse to travel where they can't carry a gun.

In the final analysis it would seem the best protection from bear attack is understanding bears and their ways, thereby avoiding trouble before it begins. Sometimes just realizing that the bears were here first is enough.

VI

Early one winter, just as the Arctic Ocean began to freeze, I watched a polar bear.

The day was cold, minus twenty-one, and a thirty-five- to forty-mile-an-hour north wind was jamming two miles of sea ice against the shore. Where one week before the only ice had been the frozen spray on the rocks, now pressure ridges four feet high filled the bay. I took shelter on a high, gravelly, boulder-strewn spit thrust from the land by the large river to my left. Ocean breakers sludgy with ice slammed against the spit where crosscurrents from the river opened leads smoking with ice fog and spin-drift. Even above the wind I could hear the grinding and crashing of river ice and blocks of frozen sea.

Although I could stay out in that terrible wind only a few minutes at a stretch, I left my shelter many times to glass the bay for bears. The only bear I saw was a half-mile from land and heading north toward the gray wall of ice fog boiling above the open water two miles out. Surely he sought seals, hunger the one urge that couldn't be denied even in such inhospitable conditions.

At first the bear made good progress across the frozen sea, but near the ice fog he broke through and plunged into the sea. He hauled out and went on, but soon his footing failed entirely. Every other step was uncertain. He'd fall, pull himself out, go on, then plunge through again a few feet beyond. He tried jumping from floe to floe but oftentimes he'd miss or slide off into the water.

The bear altered course and turned toward me, aiming for the spit and river beyond. It was not a steady course. He would veer west, then turn north, only to be forced west again. Always he tested the ice to the north.

As he came closer, I'd see him for a while, then lose him behind a wall of undulating ice. The pack was becoming more broken, and often the bear fought his way forward half swimming, half crawling. Several times he climbed out on frozen blocks and stood staring north and west. Near shore the bear fell into the battleground of ocean and river water sluicing around the end of the spit. Several times he disappeared completely. How could he keep from being crushed among the masses of battering, churning floes?

Just as I thought he must have perished, his head appeared at the top of one of those icy waves. He surfed to shore amid chunks of ice and was dashed against the white-encrusted boulders. In an instant he washed back on the outflow.

Then I lost sight of him as I struggled to stay warm, my face and hands numb and aching. Distracted, I didn't see the bear on shore until he was crossing the spit in front of me and heading toward the river. I changed positions and soon located him dodging ice floes in the powerful current of midstream. He disappeared in the ice fog a half-mile out, still heading north by northwest.

VII

Bears, although mostly herbivorous, can prey on large mammals. Researchers investigating the decline of moose and caribou herds in Alaska's Nelchina Basin first examined wolf predation, disease, and forage conditions, but well into their studies they discovered that these were not primary factors in the region's high moose calf mortality rate. Radio tracking devices showed that grizzlies—not wolves—were responsible for the losses. The real surprise of the study was not that grizzlies kill moose calves but *how many* they kill. In 1984, of fifty-two calves tagged in the Susitna River Basin, twenty-four were killed by grizzlies. Independent studies on the Kenai Peninsula showed that black bears were also adept at catching moose calves.

When the preliminary findings were made known, wildlife managers faced a public outcry for bear control, the same as that for wolf control: kill bears to increase moose and caribou numbers. However, just because bears proved to be adept predators in some areas did not mean that they were successful elsewhere. In Unit 20E north of the Alaska Range, for example, wolves were the moose's principal enemy. Weather and terrain, as well as other factors, have an important impact on predation. In many situations, a healthy, determined cow can drive off a predator, even one as formidable as a grizzly. Bears, like wolves, must test many prey animals before finding one that they can kill.

The Board of Game responded to public pressure by loosening some seasons, increasing bag limits, and reducing hunting fees for brown-grizzlies. In recent years most regulations have been liberalized and, except for banning the sale of bear parts—claws, and gall bladders, favored in the Orient as an aphrodisiac—in no case made more restrictive. These steps do not result from knowledge that bear populations can withstand increased hunting pressure but rather from a willingness on the board's part to manage less conservatively over wide portions of Alaska. The liberalization occurred at a dangerous time when funds for bear research, survey work, and wildlife protection in general were drying up. If not monitored closely, such actions might trigger a dangerous downward spiral in bear populations.

In Denali Park one of the better places to see moose calves in recent years has been the developed areas near the hotel complex and park head-quarters. These sheltered, timbered areas are equally attractive to grizzlies. One biologist theorizes that moose have congregated in developed areas because, until recently, many predators avoided humans. As park moose numbers declined in the 1980s, grizzlies seemed to become more common in these calving grounds. In the mid-1980s, one ranger on night radio watch looked out a headquarters window in time to see a grizzly kill a calf moose in the street, just a few feet from the front door. Bears came into more direct contact with people, too. In spring 1980 two visitors, in two separate instances, were slightly injured by grizzlies described by rangers as being "in an elevated predatory state." Again, in spring 1985 two more people in separate attacks were hurt by bears near developed areas.

Some bears are not adept predators; others are expert. Where one bear might be easily intimidated by a cow moose protecting a calf, another might forge ahead and make an easy kill. In spring 1986, one female grizzly and her two-year-old cub are believed to have killed eight calves, maybe more, in the area bordering the road from Sanctuary Campground to the Savage River. Biologists label this level of skillful hunting "learned behavior," a product of trial and error, and one no doubt passed on to the cub.

Neither an unaccompanied cow moose in spring nor the sight of a grizzly eating a moose is evidence of predation. The half-eaten, debris-covered deer, moose, or caribou is likely to have died of injury, starvation, or some other natural cause. Not uncommonly, bears wrest kills or wounded prey from wolves. In 1985 on the Toklat River in Denali Park, I witnessed just such an event.

At dawn five wolves chased a bull caribou from the brush across from Divide Mountain and out onto the graveled river bars of East Branch. Spread into a loose V, they quickly gained ground on the bull.

Just south of the old bridge two wolves caught the bull, slashing open his hams. With a snapping wolf beside him and another close at heel, he slowed and the pack closed in, panicking him into a series of futile leaps near a brushy soapberry patch. Wounded and desperate, he turned to charge but the wolves dodged away. The damage had been done.

With lowered tines, the bull faced the wolves spread in a half-circle before him. For a long while none of the animals moved. Then, one by one, the wolves walked away. After wading the shallow, turbid channel, they grouped fifteen yards from their prey. One wolf stretched, two others laid down, one sat and yawned, another licked its front legs and paws. The pack's nonchalance was compromised only by their long stares at the weakening caribou.

Fifteen minutes later four of the wolves got up and headed southwest toward Divide Mountain, soon disappearing in the willows. Far beyond them a female grizzly and three cubs—the same four that two days before had been feeding in the soapberry patch—were heading downstream. Some distance ahead of them a dark-colored grizzly foraged in the brush.

The remaining wolf lay down, and after a time, and with difficulty, so did the caribou. They faced each other across a chasm both greater than the river, yet thinner than gossamer wings.

Just past full daylight, the wolf, apparently alarmed by a vehicle on the road, got up and headed off after the pack. Soon he, too, was gone into the willows.

For a long time the caribou stared after the wolf. He tried to walk away but went only a step or two before lying back down. Twice more over the next half-hour, the bull got to his feet but managed only a few faltering steps.

On the west side of East Branch, the grizzly family headed straight toward the lone bear feeding at the northern tip of the bar. The sun was exceptionally warm for a late August day and not even a slight breeze ruffled the willows. The female saw, or scented, the lone bear first. She half-stood to get a good look, her cubs quickly crowding about her. Recognizing the danger, she did not hesitate but hurried her cubs away. With many backward glances, she ran her family east and into the river. There, just three quarters of a mile from the caribou, she turned and headed southeast across a channel of the river, then upriver toward the soapberry patch. The caribou saw them and got up as soon as they crossed the river.

The grizzlies crossed the braided river to its east bank and walked into the soapberries just two hundred yards from the motionless caribou. Here they dispersed. One cub grubbed at the ground, perhaps digging at a squirrel hole, while behind it the female and another cub cropped juicy berries.

As the female stepped into a clearing, her ears went up, and her head swiveled toward the bull. *She caught the scent.* She broke into a lope. The caribou turned to run but faltered. Sensing its weakness, she broke into an all-out charge; her cubs followed. The bull ran into the river where the wolves had crossed. Just as he reached the far bank, the grizzly lunged into the river with a great splash. A second later she was leaping up to grab the bull by the shoulders. In a frenzied struggle against the bear's iron bite, the bull plunged into the river, then out, then back in. His abdomen, already rent by the wolves, burst, spilling a flash of blood and guts.

For a full five minutes the grizzly held the bull against the river current, not once giving him the opportunity to use his antlers. Finally she pulled him down. In the water she tore at his neck and with her front claws slashed at his abdomen. The splashing from his flailing hooves panicked the cubs on the bank into momentary flight.

It took a long time for the caribou to die. When the grizzly let go of the neck and tore into the underbelly with her teeth, her victim again fought to escape, painting the water with blood. The cubs kept their distance at first, content to fill the air with growling but once they'd snatched a taste of warm flesh, they were back to stay.

The attack came about 9:15 A.M. and it was fully 10:00 before the bull ceased struggling. All that day the bears fed and napped atop their kill. Just at dusk, a wolf came downriver and approached the bears. Neither party made any motion to attack; the wolf was content to circle and look for scraps. The next day two wolves arrived, but the female, her cubs at her side, stayed atop the partially buried remains. The wolves moved on. Once a lone bear approached the kill but again she stood her ground.

Four and a half days later, all that remained was gnawed bone, broken antler, and a few small scraps of hide.

VIII

It is never quiet on the river. There's the chorusing of gulls feuding over spawned-out red salmon or remnants left by bears. An eagle flying low over the river flushes the nervous gulls, but the lull in the dawn-to-dusk tumult is instantly filled by the hack-hack-hack of magpies mocking fish carcasses. The bass notes in this cacophony are the growls of cubs begging shares of their mother's catch, and sometimes the growls of arguing adults. This *is* bear country.

In the quiet water beneath the high bank, mergansers and goldeneyes dive for food, while mallards, just down from the northern nesting grounds, content themselves in the faster currents. Perched in a spruce, a lone kingfisher regards the big pool where a stray cormorant fishes.

The air here smells of death, of rotting fish, and of bear piles. A million red salmon have returned to their natal waters to spawn. Now the water is fertile with nutrients from decaying flesh. Much of the run has died; the lingerers await their fate.

Maybe it's better for a salmon to be torn apart and eaten by a hungry bear, than to rot alive. Three or four big bites and it's all over. But that's not the way of things now. In early summer the bears ate whole fish, gulping everything. Now, having gained tremendous bulk from the plentiful protein, they are picky, stripping out the eggs, eating the skin, or sucking out the eyes, leaving the rest. Many bears ignore the live fish, preferring instead the putrid remains dredged up from the bottom. Submerging like whales, some bears dive down and bring up these delicacies in their paws, on the surface sorting out the choice morsels by scent.

The smallest adult bear on the river probably weighs in excess of three hundred and fifty pounds. Two scarred, old males go over nine hundred. From my perch eighteen feet up a spruce tree, I can see seven bears in a radius of less than one-quarter mile.

One swims just below my stand, every now and then stopping to reach for the dead fish it has seen on the bottom. Upon surfacing, the bear shakes its head to clear its ears of water, then gently scratches each one with a single claw.

A flotilla of gulls sails behind, crying out for scraps whenever the bear brings a fish to the surface. Several immature gulls use the same begging display they employed as chicks. Although the bear pays them no heed, they get scraps all the same. Once on the lakeshore I saw an immature eagle begging from a bear in the same way.

The worn trail beneath me is marred with a multitude of tracks. *Bear tracks.* For some reason they always seem menacing, perhaps because they're undeniably a stamp of weaponry, a coat of arms. Here and there are piles of undigested cranberries. I wonder if what I see is just a portion of the feast, or evidence that these berries offer little nutrition. Magpies fume over the piles, picking out berries until little remains.

The trail from my camp to the stand passes through heavy brush. Although I call out and make loud noises, every day I meet at least one bear on the trail, and every time it moves off. Some people in similar situations holler, "Hey, Bear. Hello, Bear." Over and over. It seems so ludicrous. Does a bear know a greeting? Or know it's a bear? I yell, "Hello, Squirrel. Hello, Mouse" and hope I don't run into another person. Since any sound will do, I often sing. (That'll do it!)

I never unsling my rifle but neither do I surprise a bear. I always give the bears the right of way. This is their home—I am the intruder.

I hope no one finds out about the big rainbow trout in the river. Too many fishermen think they own the water, and soon the bears would be gone.

The nights have been the toughest part of camping here. Although my camp is well away from the river, bears following the lakeshore pass within thirty yards. I keep my food well up in a tree and cook with caution. I know I've done well, for no bears have come around at mealtime.

It is the darkness that plays tricks on me. Every sound, a bear. In the daytime I can see a bear and enjoy it. At night, I lose my assurance. Just before dark I walk out on the beach to look around, never failing in the fading light to see a dark shape ambling along the shore. By ten I'm in my sleeping bag, my revolver by my shoulder. It's little comfort.

Only two nights out of the last ten have I slept through the night. Both nights the wind blew so hard I couldn't have heard elephants, let alone bears. So I didn't bother trying. I suppose there's a moral in that, but it doesn't assuage the anger I feel at myself for letting my imaginings take over. On the quiet nights I can't get to sleep. When I do, it is fitful. Three or four times each night I wake to yell and chase beasts away. Most are illusory, but several times heavy forms have lumbered grudgingly away. Once I heard a growl as a bear ran off. For at least an hour afterward I lay tense and expectant. *Why does the dark change things?* Like early man, I've cursed the darkness and longed for the dawn so slow in coming.

At first light I am up and putting water to boil on the rekindled fire. Next, I walk to the lakeshore, seeking the open vista. Once in a while there's a bear on the beach, more often than not, just tracks. It is always serene. By light of day everything looks so different.

Sometimes late at night, lying alone on the ground watching the firelight flickering on the tent, I feel helpless in the grip of imagination. I listen for the slightest sound. When a bear *is* trying for stealth, there will be only a soft *swish*. I know this and try not to focus on individual sounds. But often that's impossible. I wonder, is it bears we fear, or ourselves?

IX

Early people, armed only with spears and primitive bows—less than adequate bear-killing weapons—had great respect for the animal's tenacity and physical prowess. Today, some of their descendents still lower their voices in respect when speaking of bears. With the arrival of white traders and their muzzle loaders and, later, repeating rifles, attitudes began to change, as well as the balance of power.

Even now, some of the Yukon River people believe that grizzlies possess special power and should be avoided. Other Natives hunt grizzlies for meat, hides, and sport. Some, mostly the older people, have elaborate rules for dealing with bears. A few, for example, believe it disrespectful and dangerous to toss away any part of a bear, especially the claws. But such ethics are not universal. In 1972, near Cordova, I talked with two men who'd killed a brown bear for its claws only, leaving the remainder to rot.

Unlike black bears, which are hunted for both meat and hides, most brown-grizzlies are hunted solely for their skins. Admiralty Island, Kodiak Island, and the Alaska Peninsula, because they support high numbers of bears, are the areas that receive the most hunting pressure and annually produce most of the kill. Trophy hunters from around the world come to Alaska to hunt these prized animals.

Bear season is divided into two parts: spring and fall, the former favored by hunters who seek winter-prime pelts. During the fall, when other big-game seasons are open, many bears are taken incidentally by hunters seeking other game. Some are shot while feeding on the gutpiles of moose and caribou and, on occasion, illegal baits.

Wildlife biologists believe that legitimate fair-chase hunting does not threaten bear populations. Illegal hunting is another matter. In the mid-1970s bandit guides were using aircraft to spot bears, then herd them to their outlaw hunters waiting on the ground. Sometimes shots were fired from the plane to drive the bear in the right direction; a few bears were even killed from the air. One bandit was convicted of dropping explosive devices on a bear. A few of these "vacuum-cleaner" guides removed almost entire bear populations from some drainages and mountain ranges. One ring of licensed and unlicensed guides took thirty-nine bears in fourteen days. The incentive: almost $300,000 in hunters' fees. One guide booked sixteen hunters at $10,000 apiece for a season that lasted only fifteen days.

Spurred by the reports of widespread hunting violations, a crackdown in the late 1970s resulted in the arrest and conviction of several well-known guides. In one five-year period undercover operatives and Fish and Wildlife protection officers nabbed a record number of illegal hunters and guides.

Although unacceptable, it's understandable how big money might lure some guides outside the law. What's harder to understand is the motivation of the "hunters." What challenge could there be in killing an exhausted bear that's been pursued for five miles by a dive-bombing aircraft?

These people are not interested in the country or hunting. They want to take home a bear hide and they don't care how they do it. Some hunters are motivated by the desire to see their name in a hunting records book— money, or the law, no obstacle. A few of the trophies were not even killed by the claimant; someone else did the shooting.

Although I have given an account of what can happen when a bear is shot and runs off wounded, I don't think bears are difficult to hunt or kill. In the late 1960s, bear researcher Derek Stonorov met two young men who had killed twenty-three bears in one day. A cool, experienced hunter finds a bear no more difficult to kill than a moose, and decidedly less difficult to kill than a mountain goat. A bear, unlike those other animals, does possess the tools to fight back, but testing one's courage by shooting it seems a rather dubious undertaking.

Motives vary. A taxidermist I knew once sold a grizzly hide to a guide, who in turn sold it to a client who had already paid full price for a two-week trip. The hunter spent exactly one day in Alaska, just long enough to collect the tanned bearskin, then hopped a plane to Hawaii, where he was to share his two-week hunt with his secretary. The Alaska portion of his assignation probably cost in excess of $10,000. I've always wondered how he explained the tan—both his and the bear's—to his wife.

Intense law enforcement by Alaska's Fish and Wildlife Protection Division, coupled with public concern, restored order. In the 1980s, as government coffers dwindled, once again there was growing danger of hunting abuse.

Bear hunting, because it is usually not motivated by the need for meat, has many critics. In their eyes, too many hunters view animals solely as targets and things to possess—"*my* bear." If the bear is to survive into the next century, its intrinsic merits as something more than a trophy must be recognized. It is painful to imagine how diminished our world would be if bears no longer stalked Alaska's riverbanks and forests.

Several years ago in Talkeetna I sat talking with an old hunting guide who had lost his license for multiple violations. For over an hour he told tales of hunting sheep and polar bears, of close calls while bush flying. Usually he was gruff and taciturn but this day he was personable. I am sure his hunters had enjoyed his company.

Soon the talk turned to brown bears and hunting on the Alaska Peninsula. At first he spoke with a rare animation but in time his voice faded to a whisper. I had to lean close to catch his words.

"Things have changed, all right," he said. "We used to do all kinds of stuff. The damnest stuff. Not just herd bears to clients. Once . . . once we even mounted guns on the wing. Those bastards in the back seat didn't care. All they wanted was a skin. Shot 'em from the air. And that ain't all . . . we never did, but one guy over at Katalla shot females for target practice . . . All kinds of bullshit . . ."

He began to mumble and I asked him to repeat what he'd said. He picked up his drink and took a slow swallow.

"I can't believe we shot 'em like that . . . all those bears . . . it didn't seem no way we could get 'em all . . . just can't believe it . . . there were so many . . . all those bears . . ."

X

Direct habitat loss and increased human presence in bear country bodes ill for bears. *Any* proposed development, even a solitary recreation camp, should first consider the character of the surrounding country and its inhabitants. People using wildlands, no matter how careful they are or how benign their intentions, further erode the bears' survival margin.

Katmai National Park's ideal blend of rivers, lakes, and alplands supports many brown bears. Huge salmon runs plug its rivers and streams, attracting large numbers of bears. At certain times during the salmon run only a fool would invade these feeding grounds.

Brooks Camp, the main visitor complex in Katmai, is on the shore of Naknek Lake at the mouth of Brooks River, a highly productive red salmon stream. Because of its remoteness, Katmai had experienced a relatively slow rate of growth. Each year the lodge, cabins, campground, and ranger station attracted about five thousand visitors, many of whom came to fish the famed river and see the bears. Recently, however, visitation has increased to a degree that alarms some resource managers.

Bears can often be seen in summer anywhere in the developed area, as well as along the river and lakeshore. Twenty-five to forty bears intensively fish the river in late season, when the lodge and campground are closed.

By most anyone's judgment Brooks Camp is a good place to fish but, because of the concentration of bears, a bad place to camp. One recurring proposal calls for removing and relocating the multimillion-dollar development. The potential for disastrous human-bear encounters, proponents say, outweighs the cost.

"The first time I went to Katmai," said one National Park Service biologist, "I could not believe my eyes. Here were people fishing, camping, and cooking outside in prime bear habitat—the most volatile situation I have ever seen."

No one ever has been killed by a bear in Katmai National Park, and only one person has been injured. Although the park service works hard to minimize problems by offering visitor education, providing elevated food-storage caches, maintaining a fish-cleaning shack, and regularly removing garbage from the park, bear-human problems persist. Over the years bears have destroyed tents, treed people, and damaged buildings. As in many cases, it is not "problem bears" but often problem people who are ultimately responsible.

Once a bear learns to associate food with people, a fuse is lit that can not easily be extinguished. Careless campers and fishermen who allow bears to get food or fish may be writing death warrants—perhaps for bears as well as people.

On the Brooks River at least one bear learned that people meant "fish" and that a bluff charge would cause a person to drop his fish or pack—a classic example of animal behavior modification through food reward. Experts worried that one day the charge would not be a bluff.

In 1977, Sister, as she was known, then a two- or three-year-old, first learned to bluff-charge fishermen and pick up their salmon and backpacks. That year she took six or eight fish from people. In 1978 her bluff-charging technique worked so well, she managed to take twenty to forty fish. It was an increasingly serious game.

She was not the first bear to learn this technique. A few years before, just over the mountains from Katmai, bears at McNeil River did the same thing, but there the activity was short lived. Biologist Jim Faro, then responsible for the refuge, had more options open to him than did the park service. He responded by closing the McNeil River to fishermen, in effect segregating the antagonists. In addition, any bears that came into camp at McNeil were peppered with a load of 12-gauge birdshot.

Other bears at Katmai also took people's fish, but it was Sister's boldness that attracted the most attention. Whenever she got into trouble, rangers used birdshot in an attempt at behavior modification. In 1978 she was peppered with birdshot three times, once in the campground and twice as she attempted to take a person's fish. Despite the harassment, she persisted. Biologists began to wonder whether more than one animal was stealing fish. In the autumn of 1978 Will Troyer drugged the bear and marked her with a radio collar, ear tags, and lip tattoo.

Now identification was possible. Sister returned the next year with two cubs and resumed her old ways, twice swimming after people in rafts in an attempt to get their fish. Rangers were well aware of the additional danger presented by the cubs and harassed her with birdshot and cracker shells.

Designated rangers had the authority to kill dangerous bears. One of them, a seasonal employee, said that if the chips were down, "I'll shoot her. I really will"—despite the ranger's lifelong disgust with guns and hunting. The ranger was not firearms qualified and probably did not realize the importance of bullet placement or the consequences of shooting a bear.

The harassment program seemed to modify Sister's behavior, but it was a difficult time for her. In the spring one cub vanished, perhaps killed by one of the large males then in the area. In July, she got into a fight with a large bear while her remaining cub ran for cover. Rangers found the bawling cub near the top of a forty-foot spruce, but Sister did not find her lost cub until late that evening. The chief ranger who witnessed the reunion described the scene of the moaning female suckling her cub as the most moving he'd ever watched. After the fight Sister moved her cub to Margot Creek. In late autumn, she returned alone, her last cub gone like the first.

Sister was back the next year. Harassment having failed, in midsummer she was tranquilized and transplanted by boat to the Bay of Islands. Rangers removed the sedated bear's radio collar and released her unharmed. Several weeks later she returned to Brooks. (Bears have a powerful homing instinct, and a determined bear's capable of overcoming tremendous obstacles. In 1973 a three-and-one-half-year-old male brown bear caught in the Cordova dump was relocated by boat to Montague Island in Prince William Sound. Twenty-eight days later the bear was back, having traveled at least fifty-seven miles and swum seven to ten miles of open ocean.)

In 1982, a female with two spring cubs damaged a float plane, took food from an unattended skiff, and pulled five packs from an elevated storage area between the food caches in the campground. Rangers were uncertain of the bear's identity.

In 1983 a bear showed up at Brooks and as early as June 12, long before usual, led her two yearlings into trouble. The bears approached people, took food, and ripped up tents in the campground. Transplanting the bear was considered but rejected—she would return. Only one option remained. On June 14, 1983, the bear was killed. It was Sister.

Some say Sister's death could have been prevented. Critics contend that the park service initially could have been more aggressive in its conditioning and harassment and, if it could not stop the dangerous behavior altogether, at least kept her off the river and out of the campground during the peak visitor season. A biologist said he was saddened because it wasn't the bear's fault, but rather rooted in human misconduct. One ex-ranger termed the killing a waste, saying that Sister never would have harmed anyone.

Was her death needless? Consider the alternative. Every bear attack, no matter the circumstances, only adds to the general paranoia about bears. It is regrettable that one bear had to die, but a mauling, or human death, holds greater potential harm for all bears. Take the case of bush pilot Dick Jensen of Naknek, a small fishing village near Katmai, who was mauled by a brown bear on July 21, 1973. He had been busy that summer flying in support of the Bristol Bay commercial fishery but on July 20, he and his wife had time to set a subsistence net on the Naknek River. Late that day, after beaching their boat in fog and darkness, they were forced to walk toward home. About three A.M., exhausted from their twenty-hour day and long walk, they entered the outskirts of Naknek. Near a roadside cabin they interrupted a female brown bear with two cubs feeding on garbage. The female charged, savaging Jensen with teeth and claws. He fought back. His wife ran for help.

Five and one half hours later, Jensen, breathing only through a hole in his neck, was rolled into the emergency room at Providence Hospital in Anchorage. He suffered wounds to the throat, face, scalp, fingers, and shoulder.

Jensen lived through his horrible ordeal and less than a month later went back to work.

Dick Jensen was respected in Naknek and around Bristol Bay. Even if he hadn't been so popular people would have been horrified by the attack. In the days after the mauling, twelve bears were reportedly shot and left to rot.

The real value of places like Pack Creek and McNeil River brown bear reserves is the opportunity they give people to observe bears in natural circumstances. These experiences counter the imagery of snarling beasts so widely perpetuated by countless books and articles. Yes, bears are dangerous, but so are people. We have good and bad in our society; so do bears. Education and supervision, based on sound conservation practices, must guide wilderness visitors.

Denali State Park, a mix of rivers and lakes, forest and alpland, adjacent to the southeast border of Denali National Park, has as its main attraction magnificent views of Mount McKinley. It is home to fair numbers of both grizzlies and black bears.

Except for a few trails, the Byers Lake Campground, and a veterans' memorial adjacent to the Parks Highway, Denali is still only lightly developed. However, a world-class visitor center has been proposed for Curry Ridge.

Despite its beauty and peace, Byers Lake Campground attracted few campers when it first opened. Fishermen went elsewhere, and only campers and highway travelers stopped at the well-designed campground. Visitation increased with time. Soon several black bears, as well as an occasional grizzly or two, were regularly raiding the trash cans and picnic tables. Cans were knocked over, tents torn into, and campers chased from their sites. One summer, rangers estimated that perhaps thirteen black bears and at least two grizzlies were frequenting the campground. The rangers put up warning signs and waited for the arrival of bear-proof trash cans. The wait turned into months.

Despite the warnings, a few people even fed the bears and, incredibly, a wildlife photographer baited a tent in order to film a black bear and cubs as they tore into it. Just for the pictures the man was teaching bears to break into tents! (Later someone found the female dead in a roadside ditch, the cubs unaccounted for.)

By the time the bearproof cans arrived the bear problem had diminished. Some people believed that the bears had stopped coming into the campground because of improved sanitation. Rangers also knew of a few bears lost to shooters; a dead black bear was found by the side of the road. Several years later, tales surfaced of organized poaching of black bears at Byers Lake. One Anchorage man was said to have shot six bears and later sold their hides on the black market. A grizzly was killed in the campground by a man who claimed defense of life and property. The shooter said that after pouring gasoline on the carcass, he buried it to prevent other bears from feeding on it. Rangers dug up the carcass and found the claws missing—claws worth up to $100 each.

Denali State Park offers another example of the need for careful recreational planning. Trail crews developed a hiking trail along Troublesome Creek one summer. One of the rangers later told me about the bears, both blacks and grizzlies, that he'd seen from the trail. He thought it great that hikers would have the opportunity to see them fishing for salmon.

Four years later two hikers, a husband and wife, met a female grizzly and cubs there. Both were mauled. The incident made headlines.

XI

Few people would ever guess what lurks along a tiny stream that flows into Becharof Lake. Of all the rivers, streams, and freshets that feed it, this one looks the most unremarkable. In fact, grassy islets mask its mouth so effectively that it's hidden from all but the most diligent searchers. You could paddle right by and never notice it. I did, even though the stream was marked on my map. After searching false channels for several hours, I finally nosed the canoe into the right one and paddled upstream as far as possible. Less than fifty yards from the lakeshore I beached the canoe.

It was a late August afternoon, clear and warm. A few mosquitoes buzzed about; the first whitesox of the year attacked my neck and ears. After turning over the canoe and shouldering my pack, I headed west through the tall grass of the lakeside marsh.

Until I reached the firmer ground at brushline, the hiking was difficult. Where the undergrowth thinned, I stopped and stared at the trail. It was a yard wide and trampled down to mud. In the first few feet I saw the tracks of bears, wolves, and a lone pug mark of a lynx. Fish jaws and bones poked out of the muck. I fought the thought of turning back.

My view was limited by the willows and alders choking the stream. I had no choice but to follow the trail. I took the rifle off my shoulder and cradled it in my arms.

Weathered stumps and old cuttings lined the bank where I crossed on a breached and abandoned beaver dam. A few fish heads bumped along over the gravel of the stream, now only six to eight inches deep and four to five feet wide. Timber replaced the brush here, and I relaxed a little. Each time a fish head bobbed by on the current, however, I felt eyes at my back. Twice I whirled around expecting to see a bear, but there was only the soughing of the wind mixed with the singing stream.

At an oxbow commanded by stout cottonwoods, I stopped to put my camera gear together. Before climbing to a comfortable perch in the biggest tree, I mounted a 300mm lens on my camera and loaded my pockets with film. About fifteen feet up I settled in to wait.

Two hours of uncomfortable waiting passed, and other than a magpie and a gray jay, I saw no living creature, not even a fish. It was a long two hours. I wondered again why I do the things I do, why I seek such places and circumstances. I knew it wasn't for adventure. Adventure entails risk. Genuine risk. I search not for life threat but *life*. In such places I revel in the complexity and diversity of creation and see myself as only another spoke in the wheel.

In bear country, seldom do I see or meet people. I forget the notion that man rules the earth and find that the bears are equals—no! *superiors*. In these places I see, hear, smell, sense everything more clearly. Although a skittering in the leaves will likely turn out to be a squirrel or songbird, I always pay attention, always make sure.

Even a gun brings little comfort. I know about killing bears and long ago gave up hunting them. I came to Alaska because of the bears, to share their land, yet often I must carry a gun when I travel with them. At such times I feel inadequate, inferior.

After a while it began to look as though I'd climbed the tree for mere exercise. I'd hoped a school of fish would show up and entice something to come for dinner. I was stung by the idea that perhaps the bears had killed every fish, but I talked myself into believing the run was over, the salmon— and the bears—long gone. I climbed down to relieve cramped muscles. Almost at once I was startled by the splashing of a small run of red salmon finning up the oxbow of the stream. The fish struggled into the quiet water in front of me.

I changed lenses and crawled to the edge of the stream. The water was so clear, the salmon seemed to float above dry gravel. I marveled at the scarlet backs, green heads, and hooked jaws. In a moment I was absorbed.

I don't know how long I worked with the fish but a sudden silence caused me to stop. I knew the trees continued to sway in the wind, and the water to flow, but it seemed the sound had been shut off. I wanted to run to the tree, where my rifle and pack hung from a limb, but instead stood up and turned around.

On the bank above me, just ten feet away, stood a brown bear. I looked full into its eyes. Then I began to hear. The water, the wind, the rustling trees, my breathing, all going fast like a record on the wrong speed. The bear returned my gaze with steady stare. In the past, out of fear of being provocative, I had avoided looking directly into a bear's eyes. Now I could not look away. After a time—I cannot judge the interval, an hour, a second, I don't know—the fear washed away. Sounds began to slow down and register at normal speed. The short distance between us seemed not to matter anymore; besides, there was nothing I could do. We held each other's eyes a very long time before the bear turned away and walked into the brush.

My impulse was to grab my rifle and hurry away. I forced myself to wait and allow the bear to move off. Fifteen minutes passed . . . I collected my gear and headed downstream.

I don't remember much of the walk back. After righting the canoe, I paddled for the lake. In no time at all I floated offshore in calm water. I berated myself for the fear that had for a moment threatened to overwhelm me. I had willingly placed myself in that untenable position; a different outcome would have been my own doing. What puzzled me most was what had followed. I struggled to interpret the message. Later I put words to what the bear had told me.

Yes, I am bear.

I have freedom. A freedom you and your kind will never have and never know. Your envy kills us.

Pathetic creature. You think you are the greater one but your life is here in these paws. You know it. I can take it from you now or not. You can do nothing. You have no choice.

But more than real bear, I am you, the you dwelling in the deepest part of you where a wizened and dirty, dark-skinned, fur-clad man hunkers over a pitiful fire lighting a cave. I touch and dwell in that part of you that trembles in the dark at my approach, whispering of fear, of death, of life flayed from bones.

I whisper of times long past . . .

TWO

MOOSE
Season of the Painted Leaves

I

The grating of the stovepipe as the wall tent shifted in the wind roused me from a fitful sleep. Only dim outlines were visible against the opaque white canvas. It was five o'clock and the sun had not yet risen.

By this time yesterday we were halfway up the valley searching for the bull moose we had come here to kill. Today there was no need to get up. I could curl into a ball, relax, and ease my aching back. For the first time in weeks I could linger in the warmth of the worn sleeping bag and drift to the music of the dawn wind through the forest.

Later, magpies calling from the meat pole brought me fully awake. Tree shadows groping across the tent showed that the sun was high, the sky clear after days of rain and snow. Close by, a woodpecker hammered on a dead tree.

It was seven-thirty. Feeling vaguely guilty for sleeping in, I sat up and started to dress. I shivered into a wool shirt and the blood-stained jeans that I had worn yesterday. Despite two pairs of socks, the shoepacs were cold, the liners frozen. I pulled on a down vest, then a down jacket.

Sitting on the edge of the cot, I opened the Yukon stove and smoothed the ashes with a stick. From a pile next to the stove, I sorted dry spruce twigs, broke them into small pieces, and piled them on the ashes. The night before I had whittled fuzz sticks from a piece of kindling; these I now pushed under the branches. Over the branches I laid several sticks of kindling. I scratched a match on the side of the stove and lit the fuzz sticks. The fire caught and spread rapidly, smoke puffing back into the tent. I adjusted the flue, closed the door, and opened the draft.

The water bucket in the corner near the tent door had a half-inch lid of ice. I dipped water into the boil pot and put both the pot and bucket on the stovetop. As I untied the tent flap and ducked outside, two magpies skittered away from the hanging meat.

Smoke and sparks belched from the stovepipe. The tall pipe, reinforced with wires tied to the tent's supporting poles, jutted through a metal sleeve set into the canvas. The tent was safe from fire, even in the wind.

I walked to the meat pole to check the damage. The birds had pecked through the cheesecloth; swarms of black flies would appear to feed on the exposed meat as the day warmed. From a sack on the ground I took a can of black pepper and rubbed generous amounts into the meat. The flies would avoid these places.

Not a cloud blemished the sky. Southbound flocks of sandhill cranes calling in their peculiar way circled overhead. The mountaintops to the west, in sharp contrast to the azure sky, were covered with fresh snow. Below the snow line, yellow birch and green spruce mingled with patches of scarlet and white tundra.

I strolled about the clearing, stretching and enjoying the crisp, scented air. I checked the heavy moose rack and the silver tag hanging from the skull plate. The supplies hung in a tree, the extra gear was covered with a tarp. All was in order. I went back inside.

The tent smelled of woodsmoke, dirty socks, and (faintly) rutty moose. The warmth, always a surprise in a tent, felt good after the cold wind. I shivered up against the stove. The popping and cracking of the fire couldn't mask the cry of ravens sailing over the treetops. John, sleeping bag around his waist, sat up on his cot. He looked haggard and worn.

"Coffee ready yet?" he said.

"You don't need coffee. You need a transfusion."

"That bad, huh?"

"Yep. Death warmed over," I replied. "I don't know how your poor wife does it. She must not see well in the morning."

John rather crudely disparaged my ancestry but at least he began to dress. The tent now smelled of sweaty, week-old underwear.

I took off my vest and stoked the stove. The boil pot bubbled, so I poured two plastic cups full of instant coffee. John accepted his cup as a starving man would food. I splashed the rest of the water into the wash basin. Behind me John was sputtering. I heard something about "tattoo remover" and "coffee fit to strangle a moose." There were only two table-spoons in each cup. I ignored his ingratitude.

After washing up, I started breakfast. I refilled the boil pot and put it on the stove next to the stovepipe. Beside it I placed another pot of water, for oatmeal. Next to that went the folding-handle skillet, with a slab of margarine in the middle. I took half of a moose backstrap from a small cloth bag beneath the table, picked off a few hairs and bits of lichen, and cut six small steaks. I rolled these in a mix of flour and pepper, and when the margarine begin to sizzle, I placed them in the skillet.

When the cereal water rolled to a boil I dumped in oatmeal, raisins, and brown sugar. While I tended the meat and stirred the oatmeal, John mixed up a cup of powdered milk. He poured a large dose in his coffee.

The smell of frying meat filled the tent. We'd had ten days of breakfasts of oatmeal and coffee; coffee and oatmeal. Now fresh meat . . . and oatmeal and coffee. I served the steaks on sectioned, plastic plates. We both ate ravenously, cutting the meat with our sheath knives, forking down big bites. I ate four steaks, John two. Then came bowls of gluey oats washed down with my thick hot coffee. The meal took hardly any time to prepare and even less to eat. Dessert was dried apricots and prunes.

Over cleanup I asked John if he would like to go for a hike to look around the country. His "Hell, no" was not unexpected. He was tired. So was I, but a clear autumn day was not to be ignored. While gathering a lunch of cheese, pilot bread, and gorp, I gave him a rough idea of my planned hike. I told him to keep an eye on the meat and what to do if the birds or flies got to it. I also warned him to watch for bears that might trail in on the wind-borne meat scent.

Into my daypack went camera, film, rain jacket and chaps, spotting scope, waterproofed matches, and lunch. I hung my binoculars around my neck, snapped my vest closed over them, donned a blue watchcap, picked up my rifle and started out. I was glad to be alone. I liked John, had hunted with him twice before, but living nose-to-nose with anyone can get old. Free time on such a trip seldom arises until after the kill.

The trail from camp, winding through a forest of birch and spruce, led down onto the river valley and west toward the distant hills. Alone, for the first time in days, I felt the old tingle. The wilderness was mine, alive and sweet, charged with mystery and magic.

Despite the sun, I had to walk fast to stay warm. Underfoot the trail was frozen firm. Alert for any sign of life, I crunched along through a woods alive with the rustle of branches and a blizzard of autumn leaves. Nothing would hear me over the clatter of wind and trees.

One mile from camp the trail climbed a knoll commanding a view of the river valley and the two small lakes to the north. Here I left the trail, walked a few yards to a clearing, dropped my pack to the ground and began to glass, intent on finding moose in the clearings below. John and I had sat here many times while searching for his moose and had seen a few young bulls and several cows. A mile upriver, ravens circled where John had killed his moose. When the wind died for a moment I could hear them calling. Several perched on the willows, others were wheeling on the wind. I suspected that many more were on the ground, fighting over scraps and entrails. I pictured a few magpies, their long tails flicking nervously, hopping about trying to steal from the ravens.

The bluffs and slopes along the river shimmered in the wind and morning light. The lakes below stood gray and stark, frozen perhaps for the next seven to nine months. Almost at once I spotted movement in the trees near the smaller lake. It was a cow moose. She moved with deliberate steps, head up, ears erect, searching the way ahead for the shapes that bite. I watched her for some time, but only when she stopped to look back did I see the bull that followed. He was lighter than she, a tawny beige. Only his lower hind legs were the typical dark brown. If motionless, he would have been extremely difficult to see in the birch and sere grass, despite his white, palmated antlers.

I was glad no one sat at my side needing directions to the bull. Hunters fresh from urbania seldom see an animal unless it's standing in the open. Looks like the cover of *Field & Stream*. They even pay a guide and rely on another's bushcraft to find it. Over the years I've trained myself to look for a turn of horn, a section of haunch, an unusual profile, a shadow, a color out of place, a difference in texture. This talent, developed through application of energy and interest, became my most remarked upon skill.

"Man! How did you see that moose?" Usually I'd laugh to myself. Great eyesight? Me? Right. Worn eyeglasses since I was six. Twenty–one hundred, uncorrected. Blind as a bat without specs. Seeing is all a matter of tuning in, of knowing what to look for. But I enjoyed the praise. Didn't mind being Natty Bumppo. *Hawkeye.*

Directions to the quarry usually went like this: "Do you see that large spruce at the end of the stream where it runs into that pond? . . . No, not that one. The spruce, the evergreen . . . right . . . the one that looks like a pine . . . Okay, now follow up the tree about halfway . . . Move your binoculars slowly . . . then at that point swing left along that crooked branch . . . right . . . the one that has a Y at the end. It has no needles . . . Now, look at the hillside beyond it. There, just off the end of the branch, next to that small aspen . . . yes, the tree with the smooth, green bark . . . is the bull moose. Only his head and neck show. His body is hidden by willows . . . Still don't see him? . . . Let's try again. Put down your binoculars and look with your bare eyes . . . Now, then, do you see that large spruce at the end of the . . ."

Seeing how well this bull blended in, I remembered a time on the Wood River when I spotted a white patch in the timber about a mile from camp. The patch was the size of a pie plate and did not move. At first I thought it a snag or scarred tree but something seemed out of place. I set up the scope and watched the spot for over half an hour. There *seemed* to be some slight movement but nothing definite. After forty minutes of peering through the 35X spotting scope, I saw the shape disappear, then reappear. *Antler.* I knew it. I watched some more. It moved again. I called the hunter over to look through the scope. He was skeptical. I insisted it was a moose. He mumbled something about "ghost moose." That did it. We'd make a stalk.

The timber over there proved extremely thick and hard to hunt. We snuck around it and through it without seeing a thing. I felt certain a bull was bedded somewhere close and had let us walk by. We tried one more time . . . and walked right into a bull rising huge from his cover. One shot at forty feet and the hunt was over. We walked up and looked down. I couldn't resist. "A rare ghost moose."

This bull by the lake wasn't that hard to see. The two moose stood looking at each other. The cow had probably been harried throughout the previous night, or at least since dawn. The bull would have followed her every move, insisting, demanding, prodding, as only a bull moose can. But if she wasn't receptive, it wouldn't have done him much good. With her eyes on the bull, the cow lowered her head and began to feed.

Some moments passed before the bull, antlers held low and at an angle, moved forward. At the first movement the cow stopped feeding. At every other step, the bull's chest would contract, and his mouth open, breath vapor trailing on the wind. I could hear nothing at first but in a lull came the deep grunt of his courting.

"Unk . . . Unk . . . Unk . . ." He approached the motionless cow.

Echoing from a forest on a frosty morn, this traveling call alerts other moose to a bull's presence. Moose locate one another by scent and sound. When transient bulls rake their antlers through the brush, they are doing more than "polishing." Like grunting, antler thrashing can be heard at a considerable distance. A cow might run moaning to the caller, or wait for the bull to home in on her powerful musk. Another bull will answer by thrashing *his* antlers. A transient bull will go toward the sounds in anticipation not just of battle but also of the cows consorting there.

The cow watched the bull approach, then turned away. She trotted several paces, stopped, and urinated. The bull, silent now, came close to scent the flow. The cow straightened and walked away. She was safe for a moment. The bull would not follow, for he was trapped. Trapped by a solid wall of scent, a wall of fire and lust and challenge. His head went down, nostrils to the damp soil. With powerful jabs of his right front hoof, then with his left, he dug and pawed at the ground. The stiff-legged strokes worked the soil into mud. He stopped, smelled the ground again. I imagined the pungent odor. Powerful, searing. To a bull moose in rut, arousing. In an instant his head came up, antlers back, muzzle thrust skyward, lip curled back revealing lower teeth. The *flehmen*. The lip curl. The male display triggered by scent. His head moved slowly from side to side, displaying, reacting in the primal way.

The bull now lowered his head to dig at the ground with his antlers. First the tines on the left side, then the tines on the right. He jabbed and dug, then stomped and pawed, faster and faster, enlarging the wallow. He stopped, moved over the puddle and urinated into it, then lay down like a dog to roll and rub until mud dripped from his neck and shoulders. He stood up and smelled the wallow. Again he pawed at the mud before working it with his antlers, lashing madly with both palms. Once he backed and lunged at the wallow with the fullness of his strength.

The bull stopped, head up, in classic pose. Soil and moss clung to his shoulders, thick black water dripped from the muddied antlers. He seemed to hear something, or perhaps he remembered the cow now gone from sight. In a moment he trotted after her.

I got to my feet, chilled through by the freshening wind, and picked up my pack and rifle. Careful to avoid twigs and grasping limbs, I moved as quietly as possible through the shintangle above the lake.

It felt fine to be alone, free of the shadow behind. One thing about guiding, you learn to ignore the sounds behind: the jacket scraping a bush, the heavy step, the subdued cough. You are aware, too, that the man has a loaded rifle in his hands, and no matter how many times you check to see that the chamber is empty, you constantly worry. I long for days like these, free to stalk the woods and follow a whim, alone in the magic.

I skirted the lake, avoiding the thick brush and iced-over puddles. Downwind from the wallow I stopped in the scent of moose. Far enough from the source to enjoy it, I inhaled the familiar pungency. Closer to the wallow—or moose—one whiff could turn my stomach. Here, now, at this distance, the scent of musk (not unlike the smell of crushed spruce needles) brought memories of forest stalks, glimpses of beasts moving through shadow, racks scraping brush, and antler crashing against antler.

I thought of the bull I once watched in the Brooks Range. After digging a wallow, he walked to a small black spruce where he vigorously rubbed his neck and shoulders until all the branches within reach were crushed, not only leaving his scent in the tree but also grinding into his own hide the clinging scent of evergreen.

I remembered, too, the day near Ship Creek, in the mountains east of Anchorage, when I'd first smelled the musk. I thought it revolting, as indeed in full potency it can be, but here, on this day, the aroma was sweet, light, and good, even exciting. I wanted to follow these moose, stalk close, watch their most intimate acts.

The wallow was to be avoided, so I circled part way up the hill to parallel the moose trail. With the wind in my face I knew the moose would not get my scent or hear me, but I had to move with caution so that I would not be seen. If careful, I would have a good chance to get close.

I crept along until the forest thinned at the edge of a bog. I stopped in the shadow of a tall spruce to carefully study the treeline across the clearing. I double-checked every bush, branch, shadow, and shape. Just as I thought it safe to cross the bog, I saw movement, only a slight flicker, but movement all the same. It could have been a squirrel or bird but I had to be sure. I stared hard, then, *there*, at the edge of the bog under the willows growing tight against the spruce, I saw it again.

I sank to the ground and crawled carefully under the spreading branches of a spruce. Leaning against the trunk, using one hand, I worked my binoculars from beneath my vest and focused them on the spot. It took shape as the ear of a cow moose, and from that I could pick out the entire form. Behind her I picked out the curve of antler in the thick brush.

I knew from other long waits that once bedded like this, the moose could be still for hours, perhaps until evening, or at best, early afternoon. I watched awhile, then decided to sneak away to find a place where I could wait without fear of being detected but still be close enough to know if the moose began to move. I crawled from my hiding place until far enough away to stand up without being seen. Some distance up the hill I found a good place to sit. The ground was hard and dry, the trees blocked the wind but not the sun's feeble warmth. A place to sit, wait, and enjoy the solitude.

Solitude. I crave it. I love to be out like this, the wind tussling the branches, the squirrels chittering in the trees, the fresh air sharp in my lungs. Air so new it tastes like mountain water. My senses brighten. *Moose nearby.* Frost sparkling in the shadows. Blueberries to pick. *Life,* it all screams. All my life I have been an outsider, a nonmixer, feeling I never really belonged. Yet here, in the forest near the wild ones, I'm most alive.

My back and shoulders ached from the loads of moose meat packed in yesterday. I've always had mixed feeling about shooting a moose, or any animal for that matter. I'll want or need the meat—and antlers if hunting with another—but I don't enjoy the kill, butchering, or pack. The stalk is the hunt. The work begins when the trigger is pulled. But the meat is always so good, so palatable, that it alone puts pressure on the trigger finger. A winter without moose meat, or other wild meat, in the cache or freezer is like a winter without snow. When you've got it, you tire of the monotony, but without it you wither longing for it.

Yesterday we had been out before dawn, walking the river trail, moving slowly, looking to the front, rear, and sides, as we had so many times in the preceding ten days. An hour after sunrise we came to the crest of a small rise. After all the days of hunting in wet, miserable weather, we finally spotted a good bull moose. Below us were a cow and two bulls, not a quarter-mile away. One of the bulls was a two-year old, a Mulligan (nick-named for the stew), and the other was a giant, sporting antlers I guessed to spread over sixty-five inches.

We watched the three moose walk into the timber. When they did not at once reemerge, we stalked down the slope through light brush to a point near where we'd last seen them. We moved with utmost caution, taking great pains not to make a sound. At the edge of the willows we hunkered low. The light breeze carried a hint of rutty moose.

In whispers we discussed our options, finally agreeing to try and call the moose into the open. While John raked a stick through the brush to mimic the sound of antlers, I'd imitate a bull's challenge call.

Cupping my hand to my mouth, I grunted deep, sharp—an angry challenge. Once. Twice. Three times I called. At my signal, John worked the stick through the brush. In a moment I hushed him. I called again, then stopped. The seconds ticked by. In the timber a squirrel chattered. Just as I began to think the moose had moved on, from across the thicket came the crash of antlers. Grabbing John's stick, I copied the sound. The bull called, once. He was coming.

John, at my gesture, slipped a cartridge into the chamber and snicked on the safety. The bull would be close. Maybe time for just one shot.

Long moments passed without sound. I worried that the bull had sensed us. If agitated, he'd come crashing through the willows. After a while, I took the chance, uttered the Judas call, the low, lustful tones of a cow. Almost at once, to our left, a branch snapped.

"Unk . . . Unk . . . Unk . . ." and the heavy-antlered head of the bull loomed over the willows close by.

"Stand up slowly," I whispered, "and when he sees you, he'll watch a moment, then turn to run. Shoot through the shoulders as he turns."

John stood. I ducked out of the way. The bull stared across a gap greater than just the few yards between us. He blinked. Not understanding. Where was the challenger? The seductive temptress? Perhaps I gave him greater capacity for thought than he possessed, but as he turned to flee, just before the bullet struck, I thought I saw a look of resignation born of comprehension. Betrayed by deceit set against lust.

John had his moose rack, his life-long dream come true. The first thing he did was measure the antlers. Sixty-two inches across. He threw his cap into the air. "Just what I always wanted." He pumped my hand. He had me take his picture with the moose. Every conceivable angle. A whole roll of film and part of another. He could not believe *the size of those antlers.*

Instead of the satisfaction that I'd have felt ten years before, I felt tired, quietly depressed. I fought against it, didn't like the feeling, and didn't understand it. Instead of pride in my woodcraft skills, I felt sadness. We had not cheated but worked hard, and fairly, to kill this moose. It had not been easy. We had hunted each day, every day, regardless of weather. Other than the binoculars and the gun, our only tools were our mental capacities. No vehicles, airplanes, or technology. We'd sought the bull on his own ground, in as basic a way as reasonable. I'd always felt remorse at an animal's death but this confusion I couldn't grasp. Something had gone from hunting. The stalk still carried the energy-high and excitement . . . but the *kill?* Vaguely I wished the bull alive.

I'd come to judge the quality of a hunter on many things but mostly on how he or she reacted to the kill. Some people could see nothing of interest in the wilderness except as a place to shoot an animal, or set a hook in a fish's mouth. Others found great beauty, wonder, and magic in all nature. Flowers, berries, birds, bear, moose, sheep—all were equal and wonderful. I enjoyed these hunters best. John fit somewhere in the middle of the extremes. He liked the country and wildlife, but he was strongly geared one way. His elation was typical. I'd hoped for more.

The best hunters always seem deeply moved by the kill, comprehending fully what they have done. Many temper their elation with quiet respect for the animal. These are the hunters that, at some point in their lives, have come to grips with the inherent contradictions in recreational hunting. They never use euphemisms like "take," "harvest," "collect." They say "kill." They know exactly what they do and don't mask it with word-play. I have hunted with only a rare handful of such hunters. At the kill each was deeply moved, and one, a woman, cried. Each time I saw their deep emotion I walked away and fiddled with gear, to give them time alone. I knew what they felt. But I also knew that if they had to do the whole thing over, they would kill again.

Butchering John's moose was the usual labor, sweat, and struggle with an unwieldy bulk. I knew a few tricks but it still was work. John, helping the best he could, held up a leg, or pulled on the hide as I cut and skinned. The real struggle was to keep the meat clean despite the ease with which it would pick up dirt. First we rolled the moose onto its back. No, *rolled* sounds too easy. We *worked* the moose onto its back, struggling with the antlers to get them pointed down and back. Just this struggle prompted John to say, "How the *hell* are we ever going to pack this out?" Hours later, in the darkness of early night, he'd know.

Beginning at the throat, I cut a long line through the skin from neck to anus, using the first and middle fingers of my left hand to guide the blade away from the tender flesh over the viscera. I then cut into the throat, severing the windpipe. Next I cut through the flesh along the neck to the sternum. I used the packsaw to separate the bone.

Cautiously, again using my fingers to guide the blade, I cut the animal open from sternum to anus. Steam and hot smells poured from the cavity. There was little blood. I moved to the trachea, cut a fingerhole for my left index finger and pulled backward, slicing it from the neck as I worked toward the lungs. John spread the ribcage while I reached in awkwardly to cut the lungs loose. Much blood here. The bullet had passed through both lungs, breaking ribs on entry and exit. I strained to loosen the diaphragm. The carcass kept tipping over and I had to push with my knees to keep it upright. I put down my knife and grasped the windpipe with both hands and pulled backward with all my strength, spilling the heart, lungs, and diaphragm from the chest cavity onto the complex stomach. I stopped to sharpen my knife.

Next I began to cut the stomach away from the abdominal cavity. The four-part stomach, like a water-filled balloon, refused to stay in one place. One slip with the knife and the meat would have been tainted with spilled rumen. We pulled, tugged, pushed, shoved, and swore the stomach out of the way. I cut around the anus, freeing the lower alimentary tract. John and

I grabbed the windpipe and pulled the entire system from the body cavity. With a knot of grass I wiped away the blood that pooled along the backbone. The moose was cleanly field-dressed.

We took a break. While I again sharpened my knife, John took more pictures. He said that he wanted pictures of the gutted moose to show his friends that didn't approve of, or understand hunting. He wanted to show how he obtained his meat and that he used the entire animal. He also wanted to show that all the meat we eat begins this way, be it fish, fowl, beef, pork, or mutton. Rather stridently, as if talking to his intended audience, he explained that few people understand, that few people would eat steak if they first had to kill and butcher the animal. Perhaps he had a point, but I doubted many people would look at his pictures and get it.

I started to skin the moose before John finished talking. I began at the right rear hock and made the opening cut down the leg. With John's help, it wasn't long before we had the skin loosened on one side. We were careful to keep the half-skinned animal on its hide and off the ground, away from lichen, leaves, and dirt. Though I'd been careful, a few hairs clung to the meat. Before turning the moose over we severed the head from the body by cutting through the spine at the last vertebra below the skull. It took both of us to carry the antlered head away from the carcass.

We rolled the moose over, maneuvering the carcass to keep it on the hide. Fifteen minutes later the moose was fully skinned and cooling. We finished the job by removing the lower legs at the first joint. I cut away three legs in the time it took John to do one. He had a hard time finding the joint. One by one we tossed the lower legs into the brush. At this point the white and red carcass looked unremarkably similar to a full steer in a butcher shop.

With John's help, and a sharp knife and saw, I segmented the moose into eight sections: the four quarters, the two rib halves, the neck, and a pile of loose meat that included the backstraps and tenderloins. John didn't want the kidneys, heart, or liver. Some hunters consider these delicacies, but not John. A light steam rose from the rapidly cooling meat.

John, wiping the blood from his hands, surveyed the mountain of meat. Meat that would be choice and tasty because of proper, expeditious care. The moose smelled only faintly of the rut. John looked at me and shook his head. "You never answered me," he said. "How the *hell* are we ever going to get this out of here?"

I laughed. A pair of gray jays flew over and landed in a nearby spruce.

Their chirping joined in my laughter, as if to say: "Stop talking. *Show* him. We're hungry."

Sitting alone in the clearing waiting out the day, I thought of yesterday's hunt, and the heavy loads of meat packed in. I thought of many things. Food. Home. Daughter. Approaching winter. Chores that needed doing. Good times. Women. Bad times. Hunters in general. John in particular. Bears. (No matter how deep in thought, or sound asleep, I stir at the slightest sound.) Thoughts of people, places, and things seldom recalled. I thought a great deal about the moose we killed, the species in general, and the ethics of hunting. Questions. Always the nagging, persistent, draining questions.

In midday I drifted off to sleep. A while later I awoke hungry. I lunched on cheese, hardtack, and a few handfuls of gorp, washed down with icy water from my poly bottle. After ten days of Monterey Jack on pilot bread—Cheese Supremes, as John called them—I wished for something more. Wished I'd fried up some extra meat to bring along. (That's *exactly* what I did do, I reminded myself, but I had eaten it at breakfast.)

Afterward I shoved my gear back into my pack. I'd waited out moose many times before, as long as ten hours while the moose napped and ruminated. I wanted to see the mating ritual again. See the act that galvanized these usually placid creatures. While I slept the sun had slanted toward the west and I sat shivering in the shade. I looked at my watch. Two hours until dark.

Just then the call of a bull moose echoed in the timber. *Damn. I'd blown it.* The call came from north of the clearing. The moose must have moved while I napped. I slung the pack over my shoulder and hurried off, anxious not to lose them. Partway down the slope I forced myself to stop. Take your time. Go slow. The call could have been a different bull. Full of anticipation, I continued more cautiously. Moving from bush to bush, looking right and left for any sign of movement, I crept to the edge of the timber. *The bull was there.* He stood motionless over his bed, the cow beside him, both looking toward the north. I drew closer to crouch behind a small spruce. From there I could watch the moose and see the entire clearing. The air hung heavy with the pungent mixed odor of moose and spruce, the primal scent of lust and combat.

From the north came another call followed by the snapping of limbs and an angry snort. A bull was coming.

The cow whined low and took several steps toward the sounds. Her suitor watched this treachery, then took a few deliberate steps past her and into the open meadow, positioning himself between her and his rival.

"Unk . . . Unk . . . Unk . . ." In familiar cadence the bull approached. The light-colored bull grew excited, pawed the meadow, and shook his antlers. The cow moaned again, provoking him. He rushed at her, driving her back, making her wait, demanding her fealty.

A timber cracked at the far end of the clearing. Over the willows there, I could see the head and antlers of a fine, big bull, at least the equal of the one before me. There would be combat.

The new bull stood unmoving, looking down the clearing at the cow and bull. I glassed his heavy, swollen neck, the puffy eyes, and spreading antlers. One palm had an enormous rent in the upper half, a result of damage done when in the velvet. Brokenhorn, the challenger.

He seemed to ponder the situation, evaluate the moose before him. After a long moment he decided. He raked his antlers hard through the willows, back and forth, up and down, breaking limbs and tearing one whole plant from the ground. He grew agitated. Heavy limbs snapped as he worked the brush harder. I could hear sudden exhalations.

The light-colored bull, Tawny, began to respond. In ritual pattern, he rocked forward in slow paces, antlers swaying side to side. He walked to a willow and thrashed the brush with his antlers. He pawed the ground, slashed the willows, working himself into a fury.

Brokenhorn stopped to watch. Grunted once. Then walked into the meadow in a stiff-legged, head-swaying threat display. Tawny stepped forward to meet him.

The two approached in slow, rolling steps, their antlers swinging in rhythm. Step by step, foot by foot, like sumos approaching in polite but lethal ritual, the bulls closed, ready to test antler against antler, strength against strength, courage against courage. For the cow.

Seldom had I seen two such prime bulls armed with similar, multitined antlers. These heavy racks, driven before rut-swollen necks and massive shoulders, could be deadly. Because of the potential carnage, large bulls will not battle small bulls. A close-up antler display usually determines dominance. Perhaps this day dominance would be gained only through death.

Head to head, moaning softly, twisting racks side to side, left to right, up and down, the bulls stopped inches apart, trying to intimidate one another. I could see the white of Brokenhorn's eye as it rolled to fix upon the tines wagging inches away.

Moments passed. The forest was silent and still, without even the cry of jay or squirrel to break the tension. Several yards from the bulls, the cow stood watching, waiting.

I heard a sharp grunt. I looked back. The bulls had backed up, one pawed the ground. Jabbing hard at the soil, Tawny grunted. Brokenhorn responded with a charge.

The bulls crashed together, quick feints bringing the antlers flush together, palm against palm, tine between tine. In a flurry of body movement, muscles straining, legs dancing, the two sought for advantage, whirling, twisting, turning, thrusting back and forth. Hindquarters low and driving, mud and grass flying from splayed hooves, the bulls fought for purchase. Power and beauty. Grace tangled with violence.

The bulls tore apart, only to come smashing together again, neither seeming to gain advantage from the impact. Tines were aimed just inches from eyes; one unparried thrust could take an eye. Heads low, shoulders driving—parry and thrust, push and shove—they tested each other, each ready to strike at weakness.

Slowly the moss and lichen under their hooves was churned into mud. It made the difference. Brokenhorn slipped in the muck just enough for his adversary to gain ground and begin forcing him backward. With hind legs driving, and all the strength of a half-ton of moose focused behind his antlers, Tawny forced Brokenhorn back. Brokenhorn tried to stem the onslaught but could not. His legs and spine buckled each time he planted his rear hooves. For a brief moment he checked the thrust, seemed to gain strength, only to be thrown off-balance by a slight twist of his adversary's antlers. Back they came until they fought only a few yards from my hiding place.

With locked antlers the bulls crashed into the willows, separated and stood looking at one another. Somehow, perhaps by his posture, I knew that Brokenhorn was beaten.

After a short pause, Tawny charged. Just fifteen yards from me, Brokenhorn, reeling under the attack, turned to flee. His opponent seized the advantage and slammed into Brokenhorn's shoulder. He went down, crashing hard into the willows, snapping a two-inch-thick spruce tree like a matchstick. He was up in the instant and running hard into the timber, his antagonist in close pursuit.

The sounds of the chase gradually receded into the distance. The meadow was empty now. Sometime during the fight, the cow had stolen away. I listened for sounds, but other than the soughing wind, all was peaceful.

Shaken, I stood up. I tried to swallow, my mouth dry as paper. I took a deep breath and looked around. I felt the wind on my face, the cold in my body, my pantlegs soaked from kneeling in the wet muskeg. The air was heavy with musk. The sun had set and a faint twilight gathered in the timber. Ravens called in the distance.

Taking four long steps, I reached out to touch a smashed willow; ten steps and I fingered the shattered spruce. Spots of blood congealed on willow leaves. Tufts of hair clung to spruce branches. I took the two-inch thick sapling between my hands and tried to break it. I could not. I scuffed at the muddied ground, at the hoof prints filling with dark water. I stood there a long time, looking, thinking, memorizing.

In the lengthening shadows I started toward camp. The forest smelled of dead leaves, of mould and decay. I stumbled in the dark until I cut the trail to camp. On the path I slowed. I stopped on the lookout knob to stare at Polaris, the first star I'd looked at in a week, perhaps in a lifetime. I looked down at the river shining silver in the fading light, listened to its rush eastward. Then, far away north, over the tall trees, a bull moose called: once, twice, and again.

II

The first wild animal I saw in Alaska was a spruce grouse. Five minutes later I found two cow moose standing in a thicket of gold-leafed birch. It was mid-September 1966, my second day in Alaska. I walked home thrilled to the core. An hour or so later, cradling a thick porcelain mug of coffee, I sat listening to the radio. Just after I turned it on, the announcer spoke: "K-E-N-I Anchorage." I'd made it.

In a way, I came north to be around moose. When I was a child, reading stories of the wilderness, Canada mostly, the tales of moose and bear wandering past someone's cabin interested me the most. I wanted to live like that. All I could see from *my* window was smog and a stamp-sized backyard. I grew up dreaming of the boreal forest with giant moose stalking the timber. Years later, when a home in the bush was a reality, a moose passing the cabin brought a special satisfaction. I'd escaped. I lived a childhood dream. And it was good.

I remember a night in early spring, the snow gone but the weather cold. I awoke to sounds in the brush outside the front window of my cabin. Animal sounds: snapping twigs, crunching leaves, and a peculiar grinding. I got up and crept to the glass. There in the dim light of the gibbous moon a cow and calf moose stood busily breaking down the willows to get at the tender twigs and stems. The cow stretched as high as she could to reach the tallest willows; most she ate, others were snatched away by her calf.

I watched them a while before shivering back to bed, there to lie awake listening to them move around the cabin. I drifted in and out of sleep. Once I awoke to a rhythmic chomp . . . chomp . . . chomp . . . punctuated with an occasional rumbling belch. The moose had bedded down outside next to the wall by the head of my bed. I snickered at the loud chewing and beery belches.

In the morning they were gone. Only the broken willows, a pile of nuggets steaming in the dawn air, and dark shapes melted into the frost gave witness to their visit.

III

In 1969 I worked as an assistant guide for Bud Branham at his famous Rainy Pass Lodge. When we met, Bud was silver-haired and in his midsixties. He had guided for thirty-three years in some of the best wildlands in Alaska, the Rainy Pass–Ptarmigan Valley portion of the western Alaska Range.

Bud was the real thing, a woodsman first, a guide and pilot second. When he came into the country in the 1930s, Alaska was a sparsely inhabited wilderness. Almost at once he went to the bush, making his home at Shirley Lake, just off the Happy River and the Iditarod Trail. Bud once told me that his early life as a trapper, despite the Depression and low fur prices, had been very satisfying and happy.

Often I'd ask him questions to hear him reminisce about his days mushing dogs along the Iditarod. On one occasion Bud blew the dust off an old scrapbook to show me a yellowed clipping. He handed it to me and said, "They say a trapper on snowshoes cannot climb a tree." The magazine story was written by "Niska" Elwell, the pen name of the late Mamie Elwell, wife of the late pioneer Kenai Peninsula resident, and guide, Luke Elwell. The story told how Bud, breaking trail on snowshoes ahead of his dog team, was surprised by a brown bear. In the stirring fashion of the day, Elwell described how Bud's 30-30 misfired. If it hadn't been for the ferocity

with which the lead dog, Kenai, attacked the bear, Bud certainly would
have been killed. A bear out in winter is a hungry and dangerous bear, and
the story described in detail the dog's battle with the bear as Bud climbed to
safety, snowshoes and all. On the corner of the page was a faded picture of
a young man dressed in a Navy flight jacket and old-style leather headgear,
complete with aviator goggles. Pretending to read the article, I stared at the
picture, noting that Bud had aged well. Except for the thinning, white hair,
and a few wrinkles, he looked about the same, still the imposing, square-
jawed, determined man.

With the help of his younger brother Dennis, Bud established and
operated one of Alaska's most successful hunting and fishing lodges. Built
on the shore of Puntilla Lake, named for an old trapper and market hunter
who had a cabin nearby, the lodge attracted the elite from all over the
world. Dukes, princes, oil magnates, politicians, and celebrities of all kinds
came to hunt and fish with the Branhams. In the summer of 1944, President Franklin D. Roosevelt, after meeting with Admiral Nimitz and General MacArthur in Hawaii, toured the Aleutians, Kodiak Island, and south-
eastern Alaska. He spent some of his seven days in Alaska fishing in the
rain; Bud Branham, then a Navy pilot, was his guide. They fished for Dolly
Varden on Buskin Lake near Kodiak, as well as testing the waters elsewhere.
Bud remembered F.D.R. as "a good man with a fishing rod."

Bud never slowed down. Always the first one up in the morning and
the last to bed at night, he remained as vigorous and healthy as men half his
age. He conducted hunting and fishing trips that few could equal. He
seemed to enjoy the wildlife and country as much as any cheechako. "I've
been doing this for almost thirty-five years," he told me once while we sat
on a hill glassing the taiga for moose, "and I still love it."

He knew the country, the animals, and how to find the prize speci-
mens. But it took more than just hunting skill and woodcraft for Bud to
become, in his time, Alaska's best and most successful guide. He possessed
the single most important skill, the dexterity to handle people. He could be
flattering to the vulnerable, bullying to the arrogant, appealing to the loyal.
In just a short time he could make a wary stranger into a staunch friend, or
smooth over the most disgruntled hunter or employee. Unlike many a
trapper-turned-guide, Bud had a broad self-education, and what's more, he
genuinely liked people.

He also possessed an innate business sense. He promoted his operation
through movies, magazine articles, and trips to the Lower Forty-Eight. A

competent writer, he turned out an annual magazine, *Adventure Unlimited*, that detailed through syrupy prose the exploits of his hunters and fishermen. The clients loved to see their pictures and read stories about themselves.

Bud's trips were very expensive, perhaps the most expensive in Alaska at that time. "If I thought someone else's prices were higher," he told me, "I'd raise mine." A woman once asked Bud, speaking before a group, what one of his hunts would cost. He fixed on her an icy glare and replied, "Lady, I never discuss price in public. But if you have a Cadillac, you'd better mortgage it. And if you drive a Ford, you'd better sell the damn thing."

That was the first and only time I ever heard Bud use a four-letter word. But I knew of one occasion on which he had been inspired to use more colorful language. In a whiteout, a plane had crashed in Rainy Pass, killing all on board. The Army's recovery team was unable to reach the wreckage. So Bud mushed his dogs to the crash, and despite subzero cold and deep snow, he managed to collect the frozen remains. The bodies were curled in grotesque positions, and Bud had to fit them into the sled as best he could. He said it was an arduous and, with the bodies in the sled, an unpleasant trek back to Puntilla. He mushed into the yard and at once the military men rushed up. The officer in charge took a look and berated Bud for hauling one of the bodies upside down. Bud, bone-tired, hungry, and cold, could not believe his ears. He had accomplished what these men had failed to do, and had brought in the remains in the only way possible. He told me he swore at the officer and made some "disparaging comments about his professionalism.

"And I still don't feel bad about it at all."

Bud was a fine pilot, with thousands of hours in all types of aircraft. In World War II he commanded the Navy's air-sea rescue operations in Alaska. Throughout his long flying career he had seen some men killed by hostile action but many more by inability and carelessness. He'd had one serious accident in a multiengine amphibian. Thereafter he flew only in good weather. He, Dennis, and their adopted sons Mike and Chris flew float-equipped Helio-Couriers—safe, dependable, short-landing and short-takeoff aircraft. They made a habit of frequently radioing their position while on flights of any length. All were competent and cautious pilots. Because he wouldn't fly in strong winds or other marginal conditions, Bud had critics. When I heard one guy spouting off I thought of the old aviation doggerel about "bold pilots and old pilots, but no old bold pilots." Bud flew light aircraft well into his seventies in a region that has claimed many lives. He retired a winner.

In his later years, Branham became a strong advocate for fair-chase hunting. He drew up a code of ethics for guides and founded a fair-chase professional guides' organization whose membership was open only to those who would adhere to the code. He'd seen a lot of changes in Alaska hunting and guiding, and knew that the old hunting practices had to change. As first president of the association, Bud worked untiringly toward his goal.

Branham seemed to attract criticism. Success, in itself, is reason enough to attract the spiteful. More than anything else, though, his manner incited them. Before a group, Bud would speak in a deep formal manner. He never swore, seldom used slang, and before his peers, presented a rather humorless, aloof, aristocratic image: an image not at all in keeping with what he was really like. He'd hobnobbed with the genteel so much that he'd picked up some of their speech, which, from a woodsman, came across as artifice. He proselytized about ethics and fair-chase hunting so much that he seemed holier-than-thou.

Perhaps the snipers who thought him hypocritical remembered times past when Bud, like everyone else, spotted bear or moose from the air, then landed nearby to shoot. What they may not have known was that Branham had forsaken this questionable practice long before it was outlawed.

To become a licensed guide, I had to work a three-year apprenticeship just to be eligible to take the written and oral exams. In 1969 I worked my first year of the apprenticeship for Bud, the first of four well-known guides I was to work with in the three-year period. Unequivocally, Bud's guide service was the best of them all, deserving of praise as well-run, legal, and ethical. He lived what he preached.

I enjoyed hunting with Bud, not only because he was tuned into the country, but because he didn't treat me as a green employee. If I made a mistake through lack of experience, he wouldn't criticize, but simply offer "another way" to do the same thing.

"Such is life in the far, far north," he would say. I heard this trademark saying many times but never a harsh word. He insisted on splitting the chores fifty-fifty. Whenever he cooked, I did the cleanup. When I cooked, which was mercifully seldom, he cleaned up.

Branham's method was to teach by example. Before working for him, my idea of hunting consisted solely of storming through the country, relying on youthful vigor to cover the miles until I found game. Not only did I walk much more than I sat and glassed, I hardly knew how to use the binoculars and spotting scope that I carried.

It doesn't take much to ruin a hunt, just a dash of thoughtlessness or intolerance. Since most guides never see their hunters beforehand, it is a genuine wonder that most hunts go as well as they do. For a variety of reasons, but mostly because of the money involved, the dynamics of a guided hunt are quite volatile. In essence, two strangers of very different life-styles, priorities, and philosophies come together through one common interest, hunting. Imagine two strangers living in a small tent, or a cabin, sharing every waking moment for two weeks or more, enduring sun and rain, good and bad luck, in the pursuit of a very elusive goal. So much can go wrong so easily, and the demands are so great, that a truly successful guide needs to be many more things than just a good hunter possessing uncommon knowledge of animals and country. The idea that an Alaskan guide is a modern version of Leatherstocking is a myth, just as Leatherstocking was a myth. Not surprisingly, many of today's successful guides are not so much great woodsmen as they are capable businessmen and adroit handlers of people.

I learned a great deal about these complexities from Branham, a master guide.

On a brilliant September day in Helio 178George, Bud flew me, a camp helper, and two hunters to Moose Creek. Soon we were sitting on a knob looking over a vast willow thicket, expecting momentarily to see a large bull moose.

I noticed for the first time that Bud dressed better while hunting than I did (and still do) when dressed up. Not only was his field equipment the best—Kelty backpack, Trinovid binoculars, Redball hip boots—he wore quality cords and outerwear. Some of his shirts, obviously tailor-made, were a style aptly described by one of his guides as "country-western safari." They were western-cut, plaid flannel, some with a duck or deer printed in the squares. In comparison, I always felt like a hobo.

In midday Bud spotted a moose, and then, in the distance, a caribou. Through the spotting scope he judged both too small to try for. After this initial excitement, we passed an hour or more without seeing anything. I grew restless, ready to move on, scour the coulees, hills, and thickets. Bud waved away my suggestion. "Keep looking," he said. And that's what we did

. . . for the next four hours. I'd glass until convinced nothing roamed in the field of view, only to be rocked by Bud's quiet request for the spotting scope. He'd show us a moose, or a black bear, or another caribou. And always right in the area I'd just finished glassing and pronounced sterile. It grew maddening, infuriating . . . but exciting, interesting. It became, at least for me, a duel. I wanted to show my worth, to find an animal before Bud did. So I took to cheating. I'd sit a few feet behind him and look to see where he glassed, then I'd focus in the same area. It didn't work. I marveled at his concentration, hour after hour with the binoculars to his eyes. He always saw the animals first. In that one afternoon I saw more wildlife than I had the entire week before while bolting over the tundra.

The next morning we awoke to the sounds of splashing. We rushed out to see an average-sized bull moose herding a cow into the lake near the cabin. The cow waded in shoulder-deep, then faced about to watch the bull. He sniffed at the spot where she entered the water, but made no attempt to wade in after her.

We watched awhile, then went in for breakfast. Afterward the cow was still in the lake, the bull still on the shore. Bud decided to wait and see what would happen. Perhaps a larger bull would show up. For almost an hour we watched the standoff. Then, uttering a low, mooing whine, one almost of pain, the cow waded to shore and approached the bull with long, bouncy steps. As she approached, his body stiffened, his head came up, antlers rocking in display. She came to him, rubbing her head and neck vigorously against his swollen neck and shoulders. Her whining grew more insistent. In an instant he whirled and mounted her. She squatted to accept him but after a few minutes struggled free to run into the timber, the bull in close pursuit. Later that day, on a distant slope, we saw the bull again balanced on the cow. It would be that way until her brief estrus passed.

Later in the week Bud's hunter killed a bull. Not an average bull, but an outstanding bull. Ptarmigan Valley's side canyons then supported truly impressive numbers of moose. They seemed everywhere. Fair numbers of caribou, and a few sheep, also roamed the valleys and mountaintops. Back in the twenties things had been different, with Rainy Pass famous for large herds of sheep with big rams common, and numerous caribou. Moose were scarce then. The turnaround seemed a natural fluctuation.

It took two days to pack in all the meat from the moose. I packed half the meat, and Bud packed half. It took three long trips each. I marveled at Bud's fitness.

"I trust you don't mind packing half the meat," he told me on a rest break, "but I'm sixty-five now, and though I could pack it all, I just don't feel like it anymore. Thirty-three years of packing meat is plenty. Can you understand?"

As I struggled to stand up under that load, I thought, Hell, yes, I can understand.

Bud knew how to call moose. He demonstrated the different sounds a bull makes, and those of a cow. He demonstrated, too, the distress cry of a calf, and warned me never to use it when close to a cow. Despite the advice, I tried it once and ended up in a tree.

He could make the dullest hunt exciting, the smallest moose seem like the world's largest. He knew no easier animal to hunt than a rutting bull moose and took pains to make the experience worthwhile. If he spotted a good moose, he'd seem to get genuinely excited. He'd point out the prize to the hunter and launch into a whispered, though spirited, anecdote about the dangers of approaching a rutting moose.

"We might be attacked," he'd say with a look of genuine concern. Then he'd lead off on a stealthy approach. The stalk was invariably suspenseful. At the last moment, he'd signal the hunter to shoot. He was a master at building egos. He'd credit the anticlimactic collapse of the moose to the hunter's exceptional ability with a firearm. *We were saved.*

Hunting moose with Bud was just plain fun.

IV

"The ugliest thing I ever saw," a woman once said about a moose we were watching. Perhaps if I'd been new to the country, I would have agreed. Perhaps. But not now. Not after spending so much time around them. Ugly is the wrong word for a beast so well adapted to the boreal forest. Utilitarian, yes. Ugly, no.

Teddy Roosevelt, my childhood idol, found much to admire in moose. He called his political adherents the Bull Moose Party. He admired this animal's strength, courage, and serenity. Made more sense than banding behind a jackass.

Moose are built to cope with northern extremes. In summer the temperatures can rise into the nineties; in winter they can plummet to seventy below. The hollow-haired coat of a moose provides wonderful insulation in winter, yet thins out for summer cooling. The upper body is brown or tan, and the lower legs and hindquarters are chocolate—a natural camouflage pattern.

In the late 1970s a white cow moose turned up near the Interior village of Healy, Alaska. I made eight trips in three years in an attempt to photograph that cow. Finally, I made some good photographs of her. Except for brown eyes, and a very few brown spots, she was all white but not an albino. She had a calf at her side, colored much like a piebald horse. I thought the pictures of the cow and her goofy-looking calf were outstanding as well as unusual. No editor ever showed much interest. One even wrote back: "Moose are supposed to be brown."

It is easy to understand how a casual observer might think a moose a rather ungainly creature. Crossing a road, or caught in the open in some suburban area, a moose, with its floppy ears, long legs and neck, *does* look like the animal world's answer to Ichabod Crane. But just watch a moose in its natural element. See one powering through deep snowdrifts, or wading a river or pond, moving with ease where a human would flounder, and the design is clear. Or watch the long neck stretch up for willows, or submarine for aquatic plants. Observe the grace of the trot across muskeg, where a horse would bury itself. I once saw a cow moose battle a grizzly bear that was attempting to kill her calf. Her courage and fealty to the calf were admirable, yet it was the powerful thrusting forelegs that drove the bear away.

It seems a shame that so often the moose is pictured as witless. Hunters seldom see a moose except in the fall, when moose *are* guileless. What man, with a year's gap between amours, displays grace and dignity?

In summer moose are not easy to find or, with their acute hearing, easy to approach. When a moose is found, chances are it will be staring back, having long sensed the intruder.

In winter, moose are much easier to locate and are not so likely to run from human beings. Hunger is a powerful force, and often they will stand and watch a person rather than waste precious energy better used to cope with cold and hunger.

Perhaps if moose do have a weakness, it is their self-confidence. Moose have little to fear. Even bears and wolves display caution approaching moose and test mainly the young, infirm, distressed, or disadvantaged—the easy victims. Sometimes moose will watch a person walk up and not even move away. They simply have no fear of people. Even the wary ones do not understand that a man can kill from afar. Unlike some mountain sheep that have learned to flee at the first sign of human activity, moose stand their ground, waiting for the enemy to draw near. It is their undoing.

Each year many moose are killed on the tracks of the Alaska Railroad. The engine is nicknamed the Moose Gooser, but it really isn't funny. In winter moose struggle from the deep snow onto the cleared tracks and refuse to yield way even to a freight train. Exaggerated tales tell of moose attacking trains and derailing them. In reality, in winters of deep snow, an Alaska Railroad train commonly kills one or two moose each trip. But on February 27, 1985, one train struck and killed twenty-four moose in one day, mostly in the forty-one miles of track between Willow and Talkeetna. The near-record snowfall that week forced moose, struggling to survive, onto the cleared tracks, and once there, they refused to get off. In a three-day period, sixty-eight moose died on the tracks. In three weeks more than two hundred moose were killed—a record slaughter. To make the best of the carnage, some of the meat was salvaged for human use, and some of it went to the Alaska Zoo. On March 14 of that year, in what many thought was justice, a moose posthumously derailed a train at the Talkeetna depot when its mangled remains tangled in the wheels of a coal hopper car.

Mature bulls sport outsize antlers necessary for dominance battles. In April the antlers begin to grow from buds called pedicels. The growth is triggered by daylight, which somehow cues an annual internal rhythm of the male hormone testosterone. Its flow in the springtime initiates antler growth, and when the hormone is at full strength during the rut, the antlers mature. The largest antlers span eighty inches or more and with the skull can weigh more than seventy-five pounds.

During the long, easy summer, the racks, protected by their covering of velvet, develop at a rapid rate. The inner core is soft, spongy, and sensitive. Bulls move carefully, avoiding damage to the tender growths. In late August and early September the velvet is stripped away to reveal the solid antler beneath. In November and December, and occasionally as late as January, the antlers are shed.

Fresh from the velvet, and until darkened with mud and dirt, the white moose palms semaphoring from distant slopes compromise a bull's natural camouflage. In the fall, in primal urge, a bull moose must be one of the most vulnerable of all animals to hunters. It is then, when they are completely without guile, that they live up to their poor reputation.

In summer a person could search mountain valleys in vain for moose, so silent and secretive are they. By September, however, moose seem to be everywhere. It's as predictable as the turn of a calendar page. Without caution, bulls wander about, stopping in the open to call or thrash willows with their antlers.

For moose there are only two seasons: the season of birth and the season of sex. All other time is preparation. In summer both sexes fatten for the rigors of the rut. The bulls gain weight primarily for the rut, a time of great stress, while the cows prepare not only for the rut but for winter survival as well. A bull's function is to service many cows. To ensure survival of the species, it is imperative that only the strongest and fittest bulls pass on their vitality to the unborn. Fights between bulls may be ritual or actual combat, but all fighting is for the right to breed. Occasionally the loser is maimed or killed. If two bulls lock antlers and are unable to pull apart, both will eventually starve.

The move from summer and fall ranges to winter range is critical. Moose must be able to travel quickly out of the mountains to escape winter storms. A weakened bull caught by heavy snows will die on the breeding grounds.

For a full month or more the bulls expend their vitality, breeding with many cows. Winter comes hard on the heels of the rut. Many bulls enter this season of cold and famine in the poorest condition conceivable: another test. Midwinter is the time of greatest mortality for bull moose. Those that see the spring sun are indeed the strongest.

Cow moose also struggle through the rut, but unlike bulls, they feed and rest more, maintaining strength and vitality. Daily life may be chaotic, largely because of male harassment. Only when a cow comes into estrus, though, does her normal routine go wildly askew. A bull must constantly guard his cows and defend against every challenge. But a cow cannot face winter in poor condition. She needs all her strength to survive and gestate a calf, perhaps two. In the cold months ahead she'll move slowly, feeding and resting a great deal, protecting herself and her unborn. Undue stress—malnutrition, predation pressure, human harassment—could cause miscarriage or reabsorption of the fetus.

Moose function on a biologic agenda of birth and procreation, all geared to the tilt of the planet. There's only a short period of time each spring when calving must occur if the young are to survive to adulthood: a few short days in late May and early June. Earlier and the calves would die in a late winter storm. Later and the calves would not be big enough or strong enough to survive the winter. And if the pattern of calving were

different—if, say, the young were born over an extended period of time—predators would pick them off one by one. As it is, some calves die but enough of the others will be strong and defensible when the shadows come coursing from the timber.

In spring a cow with calves deserves at least as much respect as a grizzly with cubs. A cow will press home an attack if she believes her calves threatened. I know several people who have blundered upon a cow and calves in thick brush and escaped injury only by climbing a tree.

Cows with calves are not particularly fond of photographers, either—photographers with both feet on the ground, I should say. They do, however, like photographers to be in trees. Three cows, on three occasions, liked me better up a tree.

For a long time wolves were believed to be the main predator of moose calves, but recent studies show that grizzlies and black bears may be more important predators. I have seen a cow moose drive off a grizzly, but often the bears win.

Once I watched a cow moose give birth to two calves. In the brush above Hogan Creek, in Denali National Park, I saw the cow stagger and go down. At first I thought she'd been injured, but when she stood again, I saw a calf fall to the ground. I drew only slightly nearer, anxious not to disturb her in this delicate moment. I watched through field glasses as another calf was squeezed into life. It was a long fall. The wobbly cow turned to lick her tiny, reddish calves. One gained its feet for a moment then fell back when the cow licked it. The cow seemed weak, able to stand only with difficulty. Several times she collapsed. I was shocked by her frailty, vulnerability. On an impulse, I looked around for a bear but saw nothing. When I looked back she was eating the white, translucent afterbirth. I thought I knew why. She was consuming not only energizing tissue but also much of the scent that could betray her and her calves to wolves and bears. I watched her lick the calves clean, then flop wearily to the ground. In the next few hours the calves took their first few steps and grew in strength. The whole time, the cow did not rise. Later I described the calving to Will Troyer, the National Park Service biologist. He followed up and discovered that the moose stayed in that exact spot for seven full days. It made sense. Why move and put out a scent trail for predators to follow? Immobility meant that a predator would have to find a small island of scent in a wilderness sea. When the cow did leave, her calves were big enough to follow, and she was strong enough to have some hope of defending them.

The warmth of boreal summer, really not much more than a brief respite from the snow and cold, passes quickly. August sees the first frost. Sourdoughs say that the moose rut does not begin until the first hard freeze. That would be easy to dismiss. Yet one autumn I followed several bulls through the first days of September and noticed that although their antlers were polished and free of velvet, they seemed docile, tolerant of one another, uninterested even in the nearby cows. The unusual mild weather continued. Then one night the mercury plunged to ten degrees. I awoke to frost on the tent and a frozen water jug. In the willows below I heard antler crash against antler.

The rut had begun.

V

Deneki Lakes. Mid-September. Early morning.

The log cabin is dark and quiet. Outside, the wind mutters through the spruce. I'm awake, warm in my down bag on the floor. Through the window I see an ocean of stars and a waning moon. I do not know the time.

I drift toward sleep but the alarm goes off, harsh and loud. The bed in the corner groans as Bill fumbles for the alarm. I hear mutterings, the rustle of bed covers and clothing, then footfalls on the wood floor. A match is struck and the propane light flares to life. The same match lights a burner under the teapot on the stove.

The floor under me shifts as Bill moves around the tiny cabin. The door opens and closes. I nestle down away from the chill draft, savoring these last few minutes of comfort. In a few moments the door opens again and Bill comes in, carrying firewood. He puts the wood by the stove and then nudges me with his foot.

"Gonna sleep all day? Time to get up. It's already past four. Clear and ten degrees. Those big bulls are waitin' for us."

As I get into longhandles and wool pants, Bill makes tall cups of instant coffee.

"Want a cup of hot?" he asks. I do. The strong brew burns my tongue but it's what I need to get going. We've spent the last ten days together photographing moose: late nights and early mornings, searching for animals and rare light. We've been quite successful at finding subjects, and unlike most autumns the weather has been clear and cooperative. I'm tired.

Bill says he feels the same. Almost heretically we half-hope for clouds, rain, or snow. A day off.

Bill goes out to start his Jimmy van. I roll up my bag and stow it with the foam pad in a corner. As I gather my gear, Bill comes back in and pours some more coffee. We both move quietly, trying not to awaken Linda, still sleeping in the shadowed bed. Bill extinquishes the light. With packs full of camera gear, coats, and food, we go out.

Bill drives slow, taking twenty minutes to get to the Park Road. We don't speak. It's an old, familiar routine. I sip from my plastic cup and stare ahead. We both laugh when a red squirrel darts into the lights and crosses the road. To the east, beyond the oxbows of the Nenana and the ragged mountains, the sky begins to lighten. The stars still blaze but now I can pick out the form of Pyramid Mountain far up the Yanert River. In about an hour the sun will top the peaks. We pass under the railroad overpass, cross Riley Creek Bridge, and make a slow turn off the Parks Highway onto the Park Road.

Driving the Park Road with Bill is almost ritual. He's the old-timer, a one-time park ranger—some say the best ever stationed at Igloo Creek—and professional nature photographer. He's logged thousands of miles on the road since 1964, when he first came here. Usually taciturn, he'll occasionally engage his passenger in a compelling dialogue. This morning he does.

Every now and then he slows down, points or nods.

"A great horned owl nested a couple years in that tree. Johnny Johnson and I used to come here a lot . . .

"Used to see lynx near H.Q. Never photographed one there, but Charlie Ott did . . .

"Don't ask me why, but that young wolf let me walk right up to him. Evening light on Primrose Ridge too . . .

"Watched two bulls fight in the brush on that slope. One knocked the other one down . . .

"Murie lived in that cabin there . . ."

Bill slows at Mile 6, then Mile 9. Though the mileposts are gone now, we locate areas in the old way. Only a few visitors still do. Despite feeble light we glass at each stop. This morning the old haunts are quiet.

We stop again on the Savage River Bridge to watch a grizzly and her two cubs rooting on the river bars. The light is better now and we can see her digging in the rocks. Bill lights his pipe, filling the van with smoke.

I fan away the smoke and feign a cough.

"What is that stuff, anyway?"

"A blend called Irish Whiskey," he says.

"More like Irish Warfare, if you ask me."

As we drive on, he puffs up a thicker cloud.

The sky lightens, white and gray replacing the dark. Only a few stars and the crescent moon are still visible. Bill drives a little faster now. We want to be on location at first light. A distance past Sanctuary, Bill slows the van and pulls off the road. A mile away, in a dense patch of timber, near two small lakes, we expect to find a herd of moose. We know they are there. Yesterday we filmed these same moose, three bulls and nine cows. The largest, an impressive, heavy-antlered bull, had jealously guarded some of the cows. The sparring with the bigger of his rivals had been almost constant. We suspect that some of the cows are near estrus. Today might bring serious combat.

We shoulder packs and start off in single file, Bill leading. We hike uphill in silence. A hundred yards from the road we are in timber and hidden from view. Except for the wind, the bark of a squirrel, a gray jay flitting through the spruce, and our heavy breathing, all is silent. Later, the road will be heavy with traffic. Now it seems we have the world to ourselves.

Bill sets a swift pace. I like it. The first half-hour in the morning of any hike is always the hardest—especially so before sunrise. But the brisk pace gets me into the hike. I dodge limbs and snags, step over blowdowns. Walking here is hard: the ground is partially frozen, with heavy frost on the lichen and moss. It is much like walking on a soggy mattress.

We walk for half an hour. Then Bill stops. We talk quietly and decide to split up. Though we often go into the field together, we prefer working alone. We agree to meet in the early afternoon on a prominent knoll some distance away. Bill moves off into the timber toward the east. I go west. We'll circle the lake.

Before I get to the lake, I hear antler scraping against tree limbs and soon locate the bull, the second-largest bull from the previous afternoon. He's consorting with two cows. The first light of day is on the treetops. In moments it will strike the moose. I hurriedly pull gear from my pack and set up. The warm, gold light filters in and I begin to photograph. The backs of all three and the antlers of the bull are white with frost. The moose sparkle in the light.

The morning becomes one that I often dream of. The light is good. The clouds stay away. The moose cooperate: they ignore me. The bull courts the cows and I photograph them.

The hours—and the film—slip away. When finally the moose bed down, my stomach is growling. I look at my watch: 11 A.M. It seems I've been here only moments, yet forever. I know the moose will bed for hours and I will not disturb them. I load my pack and slip away to find Bill.

I hike for an hour and break from the timber. On the tundra knoll to the east I see him. He's sitting in the sun, blue cloud about his head.

"You call yourself a naturalist, yet you don't mind fouling the air," I say as I walk up.

Bill laughs his loud, quick "ha." It's an old running joke. Beneath the walrus mustache a contented grin greets me. I know he too has had a fine morning. I unload my pack, throw down a raincoat to sit on and flop down next to him. He pulls a bag from his pack and offers me a chocolate chip cookie, baked last night. I look out over the tundra. The reds and yellows mix with evergreen. The sky is a clear, deep blue with only a few white puffs hanging above the peaks. No wind, no bugs. Long silence ensues.

"Well, Willie?" I say after a while. He smiles and throws his head back a couple of times. He takes his pipe from his mouth and knocks the ashes onto his palm. Taking his tobacco pouch from his shirt pocket, he begins to talk as he reloads his pipe.

"After I left you, I came upon some interesting hoarfrost. Patterns of leaves. I spent about an hour photographing there. Especially nice under first light." He pauses to kindle his pipe. "I went to the first lake and a cow moose was standing on the bank. It looked as if she had just come from the water. Damn, I've never gotten a shot of a moose in that pond. Anyway, she was looking hard into the timber at the big bull we saw yesterday. At first he was looking at me, but soon he turned his attention to sounds in the timber. It was another bull horning a willow.

"In a few moments both bulls walked into the open and began to display, the newcomer vigorously challenging the big guy. Good light, two equal-sized bulls, and a vest full of film. I couldn't ask for more." He laughs his "ha" and smiles clouds of smoke into the air.

He describes the fight. He starts slow but soon is unusually animated. His eyes sparkle as he talks. He waves his pipe to show the slashing antlers, the thrusting bodies. He tells of their angry grunting, how the eyes roll back to show the whites. He laughs when he tells how the small bull came sneaking from the timber to sniff one of the cows feeding nearby, while the raging bulls were preoccupied. He speaks as a naturalist, not a photographer. He doesn't speak of the pictures that he must have made. He only describes the action, and the sidelights—the magpie that lighted in a tree to watch.

Bill abruptly stops talking and stuffs his pipe in his mouth. Just as quickly he takes it out and looks at it. It has been dead for some time. He rummages in a shirt pocket for another match.

We sit silent for a long time. The sun feels good. My feet are finally warm. I look off across the valley. Stands of spruce, mixed with birch, interrupt the low ground cover. Beyond the river loom snow-topped peaks. I know that before us roam most all major forms of boreal wildlife—moose, grizzly, caribou, sheep, lynx, wolf, fox, ptarmigan. I see an eagle soaring over the river.

After a long time, Bill resumes.

"I'm really getting to be a moose freak," he says. "At first sheep and bears held my interest. Not any more. I like moose best. Fascinating animals. So much behavior to watch." He chuckles. "Remind me of some people I know."

He stops as if forming thoughts, then starts again.

"Not many people would understand it, but I live for this one month a year. Just one . . . Look at it. You can taste it, even."

He picks some blueberries from a bush at hand and eats them. He looks at me, then back at the colored tundra. He laughs deep and long, his face singing. He says one word:

"September."

On the evening of September 23, 1983, William E. Ruth, 41, of Denali Park died in an auto wreck at Mile 232 Parks Highway in Denali National Park. Snow and ice had made driving hazardous. He had spent the previous week photographing moose and grizzlies within the park. His ashes enrich his favorite place in moose country.

THREE

WOLVES
Trails in the Snow

I

On a tundra carpet of autumn gold with just a hint of pink dawn on the high peaks of the Brooks Range we shot a heavy-antlered moose. A fine morning: antlers to keep and winter's supper.

The three of us made short work of the butchering and one-and-a-half-mile pack to camp. Dusk found the meat pole bending under the weight of quarters and boned meat draped in cheese cloth. A cold, light breeze discouraged the few black flies that feebly buzzed the meat, but not the gray jays that even in the fading light pecked at the bloody cloth.

Darkness came, the breeze remained constant. It was joy to be in camp, moose meat hanging on the pole. We roasted tenderloin speared on willow sticks over the spruce fire that sparked and popped in front of our drawtight tents, pitched on the old campsite above the lake. The fire, though hot, could not keep the chill at bay. It felt colder than the twenty degrees registered on the pocket thermometer.

The roast meat, surfaces burned and blackened, the insides pink and moist, tasted spicy and sharp, strong with the flavor of woodsmoke. We gorged and drank from a pail of throat-numbing creekwater, the ice jangling when a cup dipped in. Later, satiated, alone in deep thought, I sat staring into the flame and coals. The wind faded but the cold came alive. A spruce round chucked into the coals sent a storm of sparks upward into the ink of the new-moon sky. The ragged peaks to the north, lost earlier in the blackness, loomed now against a growing green backlight. In minutes the light grew into distinct bands: three immense waves flashing south, ghosting the ground in fevered light.

Horizon to horizon the sky writhed with descending patterns so intense it seemed that I could reach out and touch them. At times the aurora masked the outlines of Orion and the Great Bear, the light fading here, then there, only to brighten with a rush and snap elsewhere.

How long the wolf had been howling before I heard it, I couldn't say. Old sourdoughs speak of *hearing* the aurora. Perhaps in this time and place the cry seemed part of the moment and was missed. Only when the second wolf, then a third, began to howl, did the hair on my neck prickle and chills flutter on my spine. I came wide-eyed to my feet, staring north over the tall aspens, straining to see shapes coursing the muskeg. From out over the tundra and lake the wind blew through the willows, bringing the howling sharp and clear. Four, five, perhaps six wolves moaning in the night. I dropped wood on the fire and stood tense, watching, listening, the wind-tears streaming on my cheeks. Still louder came the howling, long, deep notes sung in unison. Now, for sure, closer.

All at once they stopped, leaving the night, the mother of fear and mystery, to the snap of fire in wood and sky. I waited. Silence. I looked up. The aurora had gone, the stars again blazed crisp.

Later, shivering in my sleeping bag, I tried to sleep, but despite the protests of my aching muscles, I lay awake listening to every twig and wind sound, my eyes wide to the stars and cosmic light.

A few mornings later I sat on the rocky knoll behind camp, glassing the flats beyond the lake. Its riffled water sparkled in the first light. Just as the light slanted full onto the tundra, two flashes of white streaked from the timber. A white wolf and a gray ran full out into the daylight as if pursuing something. Near the lake they slowed to a walk and came softly through the reeds to the strand, stopping side by side to drink.

I shall never forget that image. The shimmering water, the dancing reeds, and the two wolves, tails and fur curling in the wind, all bathed in amber dawn light. So indelible the image, I can still see the white wolf raise its head to scent the air, water dripping silver from its muzzle. I can see the wolves turning to nuzzle each other with tongue-lolling, laughing jaws. Then they turn away from the lake to dart back across the tundra and into the timber.

Moments like these forever charged that place with a special excite-ment. East of a fork of the Koyukuk River, on the southern edge of the Brooks Range, that valley, which I found quite by accident, came to be known to us as the Wolf Fork. For there, in that remote place, on an unnamed tributary, I stumbled on a wolf denning valley—a place where wolves bred, whelped, reared their young, and taught them to hunt.

To the north and east of the Wolf Fork rise the high peaks, and to the south and west the foothills of the mountains Bob Marshall called the Range of Blue Light. North and west on the ridgelines Dall sheep roam. In the spruce stands and willow thickets live moose, some bulls with outsized antlers spanning seventy inches or more. Although shy and seldom seen, grizzlies wander both alpland and forest, their tracks the only usual sign of their passing. (Sometimes late at night, sounds outside the tent hold imagi-nary menace. Shadows turn into bears.) Ptarmigan, spruce grouse, and snowshoe hares live here, as well as the grayling and char that fin the clear waters.

People also live seasonally in that seventy-five-square-mile valley. Just below where the Wolf Fork storms through a narrow gorge, two partners and their summer hands slave after the gold that collects in quantity on the shallow bedrock. Except to kill an annual moose, and shoot bears that wander into camp, the men grub the gravel too compulsively to pay much attention to their wild neighbors.

The Wolf Fork was remote and seldom-visited until an army of men came to build a span of oil pipeline on the very western edge of the valley. The event would change forever not only the valley but Alaska as well. The army of boomers and stiffs, by accident and design, changed the ways of wildlife, offering food sources too tempting to resist. Shy grizzlies grew bold, and losing all fear of humans, they menaced pipeline crews, remote villages, and mining camps. The iron and steel tornado passed, but the bears stayed, boldly entering any camp or habitation, seeking the easy pickings that sealed their doom.

And the miners dealt with them. On the Wolf Fork, as elsewhere, grizzlies that came into camp were erased with the crack of gunfire. One summer the miners shot eight grizzlies, bears turned dangerous by their proximity to man. The bears were buried in deep holes dug by D-8 Cats. Two years later, there were no bold bears to shoot.

Across all the valley and beyond ran the wolf pack. On almost any night there you could hear the wolves singing. Sometimes we'd see them, pups and adults alike, coursing the tundra or ghosting through the woods. Just for the chance to watch, I searched for the den. My hunt brought close contact, but the den remained an elusive prize.

The first time I saw a wolf there, Vic Zarnock and I were waiting on the edge of a gravel strip for the plane that would take us back to Fairbanks. We'd been hunting sheep in the mountains for a week, and Vic had killed an eleven-year-old, loose-toothed ram. I was dozing, leaning against my pack of gear and meat, when Vic pointed and said: "Look." There, not forty yards away, stood a vole-red wolf. It held our gaze a moment, then turned and paced down the gravel bar. Vic jumped up to rummage through his backpack for his instant camera. Finding it, he hurried off through the brush parallel to the wolf. A moment later he emerged from his crashing "stalk" and with a loud metallic *click* startled the wolf into a lope. Vic trotted back, a satisfied smile on his face. "Got him," he said, flipping the camera back into his pack. I could not speak.

By the following autumn, additional sightings had confirmed that many wolves lived in the valley. One day that second fall I got more than the usual fleeting glimpse. I'd climbed a bluff behind the miners' camp to glass the remains of a moose the men had killed for winter's meat. The gutpile was hidden behind a line of willows, but circling ravens and darting magpies gave it away. In the afternoon, returning to the lookout from a hike, I glassed again and this time spotted three wolves approaching the kill.

The wolves were in vigorous action, running in and out toward the remains. They'd dart in, then leap away, all acting in concert. In graceful high leaps and bursts of speed they seemed to taunt something. Then they came together and stood still. Moments passed with little movement until one wolf leapt into the brush; the others stood quiet, watching. All at once the two erupted into action, charging into the brush at a full run. At equal speed all three wolves rushed back into the open with a grizzly in full pursuit. One wolf limped and fell behind, but just as the bear seemed close enough to pounce, the other wolves darted in long enough to allow the injured wolf time to get away. The chase went for many yards before a second bear came running from the brush. The fractured pace allowed the second grizzly to catch the first, but instead of joining forces to attack, both bears stopped to watch the wolves sprint out of sight.

In the running fight, the wolves never really closed with the grizzlies, but only came near. A grizzly may be quick, but no bear can match a wolf.

The grizzlies stomped around for a while, bluff charging in the wolves direction but soon beelined back to the kill.

Several times I saw and heard the Wolf Fork pack, usually at a distance but sometimes at close quarters. Once, hiking with John Thuma, I came face to face with a white wolf. We stopped to stare. The wolf stared back a moment before slipping away into the willows.

No matter how often one sees wolves—it is never *often*—the response is invariably the same: surprise mixed with confusion, then adrenalin-rush. First: "Oh, a *dog*." Then: "No, you idiot, that's no dog, that's a . . ." The excitement is intense.

That was the way of most close contact. A brief look, then nothing. One of the miners, though, had a slightly more interesting experience. On that same trail, near the same spot, he too came on a wolf that moved quickly into the brush. He walked on. Looking back, the miner was startled to see the wolf following. If he hurried, the wolf hurried. If he slowed, the wolf slowed. A strong man more accustomed to the roar of diesel engines than the silent glide of a wolf, he later admitted to fear. ("I didn't know what the damn thing was going to do.") The situation twisted wildly out of control when, turning a bend in the trail, the miner saw a grizzly walking toward him. (*"Good lord."*) Into the brush and up a spruce he climbed. The snapping branches startled both wolf and bear. Fifteen feet up he looked back to see the two animals staring at him. What he felt when the grizzly suddenly bounded toward him, he didn't say, but he climbed until there was no more tree to climb.

The wolf went the opposite way when it saw the bear charge. The grizzly evidently never saw the wolf. He muttered and paced below the tree until near dark, then wandered off, allowing the miner to descend. The miner said the walk back in the dark aged him ten years.

One morning I saw six wolves. Don Schumaker and I had stayed in camp late that day, waiting for the windy rain to slacken. About nine o'clock the weather started to improve. While Don wrapped a swollen ankle, I climbed the lookout knoll by camp. Almost at once howling began, seeming to come, as it often does, from near, then far, then near again. Time and again I looked out over the bluffs, tundra, and river flats, yet I couldn't locate the wolves.

Long after their song began, I spotted the wolves a half-mile away to the south in a spare black-spruce thicket that sloped down to the river. Two adults with three nearly grown pups pointed muzzles skyward: five sounding like twice the number. For twenty minutes they howled, then stopped. The largest wolf, a gray, walked away from the pack and sat watching to the east. All the wolves seemed to listen for a while, but in time the other adult joined in a rough-and-tumble with the pups, tossing and wrestling on the lichen and moss.

Minutes later the gray adult jumped up and trotted east, head low, tail wagging briskly. The others stopped to watch. A huge black wolf came rushing toward them through the scrub brush. The gray and the black met, the gray fawning. The pups were soon on the pair, two crawling forward to rub against the black's neck and chest. The other adult did not approach. The five pressed tightly together, jostling and nudging with tails waving. The big wolf leaped from the mêlée and ran off uphill, leading the entire pack from sight.

I have never witnessed the wolves make an actual kill, though once through the spotting scope I saw four wolves chasing a cow moose. I imagine that the cow escaped, for she seemed to be pulling away from her pursuers as they went from view.

Once I stumbled on an hours-old moose kill. The bull's hams were rent and bloody, and great chunks had been torn from the viscera. Not at all a clean kill: the moose had bled to death. I backtracked a quarter-mile and lost the trail where the moose had come splashing from the river. Blood-stains painted the sand and rocks. Wolf tracks blended with splayed moose prints. On an incline where the bull had stumbled, I found large stains and tufts of hair.

I bent over the moose and traced the lacerations in the hide and muscle, putting my hands into the wounds. I rubbed the dry blood away to feel the jagged edges of ribs bitten through. It seemed impossible that teeth could shear half-inch moose hide, tendon, and bone. I groped into the chest, passed where the great lungs once had been and cut loose the remains of the heart. Big slices were missing from the lower half, only the tops of the atriums were left. The heart was dry.

I have not been back to the Wolf Fork in six years. From what I hear, there's no reason. The new park, Gates of the Arctic, forced the hunters east into the wolves' denning valley. The country changed. The moose went fast, the wolves soon after. I'm sure some animals remain but it wouldn't be the same. I choose to remember it as it was: big racks moving through the timber and ethereal howls rising under auroral curtains.

II

Twice in Denali National Park I've seen wolves stalk big game. The first time the intended victims, two bull caribou, narrowly escaped. On the second occasion, five wolves attacked and wounded a lone bull caribou, but a grizzly with three cubs came along to take the kill away.

In early afternoon on a cold, windy, overcast day, driving east on the Park Road, I stopped on the down side of Stony Hill to look for caribou. It took will power and a heavy parka to sit in that wind long enough to peer through a spotting scope. The pain was worth it when I spotted what at first looked to be a sheep in the alplands above Bergh Lake. At a higher power the variable scope revealed a light gray wolf. A moment later, a darker wolf came trotting behind. At first glance, the leader seemed to be a pup, but when the two drew together, they both looked to be adults. I watched the leader bed down while the other hunted squirrels. Nose to the ground, it sniffed at the parka squirrel dens that pocked the slope. I dismissed as futile the idea of a stalk for photographs and stayed put with the scope and binoculars. It proved to be a wise decision, for soon the pair started downhill. They hadn't gone far when they stopped short, turned, and raced back uphill. Something in the lowland below seemed to have frightened them.

The wolves quickly disappeared behind a ridge where yesterday I'd seen a band of ewes and lambs. Half an hour passed with no glimpse of the wolves. They could have slipped away unseen, or curled up for a nap in any of a dozen places. While glassing for them, I saw hikers approaching the road. Perhaps unknowingly they had alarmed the wolves.

Then up high, higher even than the gyrfalcon nest, the wolves trotted into view, moving east across the talus slopes. They soon rounded the summit and went from sight. I jumped in the truck and headed down onto the flats of Highway Pass. I found a roadside pullout and saw the wolves moving surprisingly fast, angling downhill over steep slopes and broken rock.

The light wolf, the leader, trotted into a gully while the second re-mained above, statue-still, staring toward the east. She—I called the leader a female though I have no way of knowing—limped slightly, favoring her left front leg. (Four years later, Dr. L. David Mech radio-collared a male wolf with a malformed left front foot. Mech believed it to be the Alpha-male of the pack that hunted this area.) Many times she loped along on only three legs. She paused at a willow thicket, perhaps to hunt ptarmigan. Her companion watched from above as she cast through the willows without success. She left the gully to head east again, low enough now to be on tundra instead of rock. The second wolf ran hard to catch up. On the rock and dirt the wolves were difficult to see, but on the green slopes they stood out as bright as Dall sheep.

At one point, perhaps when resting my eyes from the strain of glassing mile-distant animals, I noticed two caribou half a mile in front of the wolves. One bull was an immense specimen that I had photographed two days before. He sported a huge set of antlers, the tops palmated somewhat like the rack of a moose. I'd seldom, if ever, seen a larger caribou. The smaller bull had blood-red antlers. When I had photographed him earlier, he had been in velvet. The big bull fed quietly in a gully, his companion bedded on the slope above. Although the white mane of the big bull could easily be seen, I knew by the lay of the land that the caribou were hidden from the wolves. Yet the one wolf had stared in the right direction.

▶ *The most dangerous of all bears is one accustomed to obtaining human food and garbage. Proper handling and disposal of edibles will prevent many difficulties.*

▼ *In the early 1960s this plane, outfitted with a semiautomatic that could be fired from the cockpit, was used by the state to kill brown bears.*

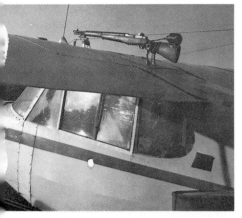

▼ *Bull caribou test one another with antler displays and jousts. On rare occasions pairs will lock antlers and be unable to extricate themselves; slow starvation is inevitable.*

◄ *Dall sheep populations were devastated by market hunting during the first years of this century, when sheep meat sold for about twenty-five cents per pound. Commercial hunting ended in 1925 but the populations continued to decline until midcentury.*

▼ *Only those people who have never looked into the eyes of a bear or wolf think that animals cannot talk.*

▲ *In 1948, in Cold Bay, Robert C. Reeve killed what was then believed to be the largest bear — in body size — ever taken in Alaska. Today, largely because of hunting, few bears attain such prodigious size.*

◀ *Victor Zarnock backpacks a heavy load out of a drainage in the Brooks Range. A day later, as we sat waiting for our plane, a wolf sauntered by.*

▼ *The tundra wolf is an animal of legend and mystery, fact and fancy, love and hate.*

▲ *Throughout most of the year, large bulls remain solitary, or at best keep company with another bull. In early autumn, the rutting season begins and summer habits fall away, bulls traveling in search of cows, which they locate by scent as well as sound.*

◄ *A wall tent fitted with a wood stove provides shelter, warmth, and comfort, not only a camp to hunt from but often a home in the high bush.*

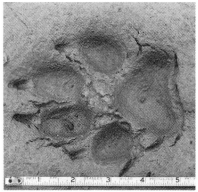

▶ *Pressed into the mud of a Brooks Range streambank, the five-inch-long track of a wolf gives evidence of the passage of North America's most capable predator.*

◀ *A twelve-year-old ram is considered old, but the oldest Dall ram killed by a hunter in Alaska was fifteen. Unlike antlered animals, which shed their headgear annually, sheep retain their horns, which grow a few inches each year. Large horns are usually the product of long life, but few sheep survive long enough to grow horns this size.*

▼ *In November and December, as the harsh northern winter takes firm grasp of the country, Dall sheep gather for the rut. Thick coats and layers of fat protect sheep from the elements, but the energy drain takes its toll, especially on the rams. Many of the older ones die in the cold darkness of the arctic night.*

▲ *On the North Slope of the Brooks Range, John Hewitt watches the passage of a herd of caribou numbering in the thousands. Lightweight food and a small tent offer the biker mobility, as well as the challenge to follow where the wind and the caribou go.*

▶ *Diminishing daylight triggers hormonal changes within moose. By the second week in August, bull moose begin to shed the velvet covering on their antlers and are ready for the dominance displays and battles of the September rut.*

▶▶ *Fleet caribou prefer open tundra and mountains where they can see potential enemies at a distance. Bothered by countless hordes of biting and burrowing insects, caribou also find relief in these windy, open places.*

Both wolves were now, by design or accident, heading straight toward the bulls.

I expected to wait awhile for the wolves to cover the half-mile, but a faster pace soon brought them to the edge of the gully where both caribou were now feeding. The wolves stopped at the crest, two hundred yards from the caribou. The wolves drew together and sat down, flanks touching. Planning? Communicating?

The leader went forward, creeping low to the ground. She went a few yards then stopped, belly down. A second passed, then she went forward again. She continued the pattern: a low creep, a momentary pause on her belly, then forward a few more yards. Her companion followed, walking upright but holding his head down. Ten yards. Twenty yards. Thirty yards closer . . . then they charged, covering the ground with giant strides. The smaller bull saw them almost at once, leaped high, and raced away to the east. The wolves quickly were out of view in the gully into which the big bull had fled. The seconds ticked away. Had they caught him? Had the wolves made a kill?

Head high and antlers back, the bull dashed into view over a ridge and plunged straight down the rocky slope. The wolves followed shockingly close, perhaps just twenty or thirty feet behind, flanking the bull. One stumble or faltering step and he would have felt their bite. Going down the slope he picked up speed and began to widen the gap. The wolves suddenly stopped and watched him race away.

The female, leader in the stalk and chase, watched but a moment then turned to race back uphill. The other, smaller bull stood a few hundred yards away. As soon as he saw the wolves he began running. Without trace of a limp, the white wolf put on an incredible burst of speed, leaving the other wolf behind. She seemed pneumatic, rocketing across the tundra like some giant peregrine in a stoop. Her partner trailed well behind. The gap between hunter and prey narrowed as the bull raced behind a low hill, his pursuer just one hundred and fifty yards behind . . . and gaining. Both wolves soon disappeared behind the hill.

When they emerged, the bull had turned toward the road—directly toward me—with the two wolves close behind, the leader to the bull's right, the other wolf a hundred yards back to the left. Nearly to the road, the bull swerved west, heading downriver toward Bergh Lake. Here the wolves split up, the female still in pursuit, the male stopping to watch.

In the distance I saw the caribou still running strong as he neared Bergh Lake. Upstream, trotting along slowly, tongue dangling from slack jaws, his pursuer had all but quit. At a still greater distance trailed the second wolf. By Bergh Lake, about a mile from where the chase began, I lost sight of all three animals as they entered heavy brush.

I turned the truck around and drove up Stony Hill. From there I could see the caribou near Bergh Lake. He again was in flight, a wolf—I could not tell which one—close at heel. The bull came to the lake and raced right in, breasting the wind-driven whitecaps with powerful strides. The wolf hesitated, then it too jumped in. Very soon, though, the wolf turned around and struggled back to shore, where it was met by its partner. The bull swam easily to the east bank, climbed out, shook off the water, and looked back. Both wolves stood together on the west bank looking off at the distant caribou. In a few moments they ran off to the west and out of sight.

For over an hour I watched the bull. He'd stand for a while, then lie down, but always looking to the west. He seemed to be resting, conserving energy for some future flight, but for now he had survived.

The caribou was the second animal I had seen escape a predator by taking to the water. Once I had seen a cow and calf moose elude a grizzly by swimming a lake. The bear swam better than the wolf but still was no match for the moose. The caribou is the best swimmer of all, his hollow-hair coat buoying him up like a cork on the waves.

In the two hours I'd watched the wolves, they had covered more than five miles of rugged country, most of it at a run. Several things still confound me: why had the wolf limped when it walked yet been able to run so well? How did the wolves choose their prey? They were close to the big bull yet had given him up to chase another that was over a quarter-mile away. Most puzzling of all: Why, with all the possibilities, did the caribou run toward Bergh Lake? Accident, or design? Bergh Lake sits in an almost perfect cul-de-sac . . . the water offered the only escape.

III

The howling of wolves never fails to stir ill-defined emotions within me. But what does it do to other animals? How do they respond? I often wondered; one autumn I found out.

I had spent a morning photographing a large bull moose consorting with four cows. About ten o'clock they bedded down in a spruce thicket bordering a pond. I sat down to wait them out and eat my breakfast, a frozen peanut butter sandwich. I'd just taken a bite when the first howl drifted over the taiga. The moose jumped simultaneously from their beds to move *toward* the howl, which came from a knoll about one-half mile away. The moose took several strides into the open to the edge of the timber, where they could look out over the willows beyond the pond. I abandoned my sandwich and crept closer. I studied the heft of the bull's antlers and could not imagine a wolf challenging him, or even attacking one of the cows in their autumn prime.

The howling died away but the moose remained on guard. After several minutes, from behind us, on the river to the east, another wolf howled. The one on the knoll answered. The moose did not look around but kept watching the knoll. I looked over *my* shoulder.

All at once, all five moose looked slowly to their right. About two hundred yards away a gray wolf walked from the timber and headed across the flat toward the knoll. The willows were thick and the wolf was forced to jump from clearing to clearing, much like a rabbit in high brush. I got an extraordinary look at this graceful creature as it crossed the flat. But as soon as the wolf started up the knoll, I lost sight of it in the brush. The five moose stood for several minutes, then one by one they began to feed. They appeared undaunted by the wolves, but as they fed they moved east, eventually crossing the river to the timber on the east side of the valley, putting both water and distance between themselves and the wolves. They had no escape. They had to face whatever came skulking through the taiga. They could not climb a tree, or fly away, or close a stout door: distance was their only protection. As they disappeared into the woods, only the far cry of a raven rent the silence.

IV

In the midsixties, fresh from California (where the word "wolf" referred only to the two-legged variety), I couldn't wait to see a wolf, or hear howling. All my knowledge of Alaska and wolves stemmed from reading natural sciences, the fiction of Jack London, and the poetry of Robert Service. I admit coming north with all the cheechako's misconceptions of the country and its wildlife.

One of my favorite books had been Lois Crisler's *Arctic Wild.* Even as a teen I found the writing powerful and evocative. I remember well the

Crislers' descriptions of wolves and wolf behavior, especially the passage depicting the return to the wild of their quasitame wolves, Silvermane and Trigger. I shared their dilemma when their time in the arctic ended and, knowing that their other tame wolves could not fend for themselves, they faced the choice of taking them to civilization or killing them. The Crislers took the wolves south.

(Many years later, after I'd lived in Alaska a few seasons, I learned the fate of Silvermane and Trigger. I met the man who had killed them. The winter after the Crislers left, a veteran bush pilot was flying in the Brooks Range, just a drainage away from where the Crislers had their cabin. He saw a pack of wolves on the river below. He made a quick turn and landed within rifle range. To his astonishment, the wolves came bounding up to the plane. Only later did he realize he'd killed the Crislers' wolves.)

In part because I held such high expectations, my first encounter with wolves seemed bland. On a calm, subzero day in winter 1966, near Buffalo Mine, I followed a frozen creek, terraced with beaver dams, into the Talkeetna Mountains. Far from the traffic on the Glenn Highway, my senses bright from the cold and the roar of complete silence, I wandered along, noting the sign of beaver, the track of moose, otter, and ermine. Red squirrels skittered in the treetops, and once a huge cow moose rushed off through the snowy timber. In a copse of birch where the creek narrowed and the beaver had yet to work, a trail sliced across the ice. There, burned through the powder snow to the black ice below, was the track of a wolf. A perfect print: the pad, toes, and nails in sharp relief. And *huge*. Much larger than expected. *Five inches long*. I'd seen smaller black bear tracks.

I followed the winding trail through the tall birch into the spruce and up a slope, fighting the snow-laden brush to a clearing on the ridge. The wolf had paused there in the open to scratch out a shallow bed. The Talkeetnas rose sharp to the west, the white broken only by brown and black rock and the gray skirt of brushline. Behind me, to the east, the Chugach Range reared from the timbered Matanuska River bottoms. I looked in all directions but saw no movement. No moose. No birds. No sound even, not even the jabber of a squirrel. A total silence I'd never before experienced. I strained to hear a howl or see the wolf stalk from a distant covert. Time passed. I stood motionless, aware of the vapor rising at each breath and the numbness in my fingers. Even the slightest rustle of clothing seemed overloud.

From the highway hidden in the spruce and cottonwoods six to seven miles away the sudden roar of a Jake brake on some diesel tractor broke the spell. I sighed, shrugged off the cold, and started down the hill. But the wolf *had been there.*

It wasn't until some time later that my phantom took form. One year I worked for Bud Branham, the famous fair-chase guide, in his Rainy Pass region. He and I, with two hunters, were hiking a brushy draw near Sheep Lake when, off to the west on the highlands near Rainy Pass itself, the howling of wolves stopped us cold. "A hunting pack, maybe six," Bud whispered to us in a deep, melodramatic tone. (He was like that.) I pictured a wolf pack, tongues slavering, howling out their blood lust as they pursued some unfortunate caribou. (I admit to having read too much Jack London. Wolves don't howl when in pursuit of prey, but that *was* the image that came to mind.) The howling washed my weariness away, brightened all my senses. At once I was aware of the cool breeze on my cheeks, the crisp September air, the colors of autumn. I forgot the pull of the pack and heft of the gun. I heard the willow leaves rustling, the redpolls talking, the water chuckling over the stones. And over all the howling, new and exciting.

We set up the scope on a tundra knob and glassed and glassed, and finally Bud found a single wolf trotting across a distant ridge. Before it went from sight, we each got a brief look, a glimpse I'll never forget.

The following winter a top bush pilot flew me through the Alaska Range and back home from the Big River. We flew through Ptarmigan Pass, south of Rainy Pass, and up the valley toward Sheep Lake. Almost in the exact spot where I had been when I'd heard the wolves the fall before, we spotted a pack. At four hundred feet above ground level my pilot made flawless tight turns over the wolves so that I could get pictures. Almost at once the wolves started to scatter—they'd learned to fear airplanes. He leveled out, made a sharp downwind turn, pulled on full flaps and set the Cub down between the drifts and onto the concrete-hard snow next to the wolves. We slid to a stop. He pushed the door up and I struggled out, camera in hand. In the sudden cold and silence we watched the four black wolves and three grays sprint over the drifts and out of sight. Though I'd glimpsed wolves before, the first on the Taylor Highway, a straggler behind migrating caribou, this pack running together spoke of something different—teamwork. I'd seen evidence of coyotes teaming up to prey on sheep at lambing time, but this pack running over the drifts brought into focus the concept of cooperative hunting, the group a more formidable predator than the individual. Could any moose, already floundering brisket-deep in heavy snow, protect itself from these agile wolves?

The wolves were soon gone over the drifts. The valley echoed with howling as the scattered pack regrouped. By the time we freed the skiis from the snow and were airborne, the pack had disappeared into the willow flats. A mile away we saw a moose mired up to his chest in a drift. The wolves had gone the opposite way.

The next autumn, after working with the Alaska Department of Fish and Game and spending my free time photographing wildlife—including a session with a black wolf in Denali Park—I worked for an outfitter on the north side of the Alaska Range. Late one afternoon, after an unusually early and heavy snowfall, I led a packtrain loaded with moose meat through the passes near Dick Creek, a tributary of the Yanert River. In the narrow canyon below the pass, a raging wind made me hunch deep into my parka. I missed seeing the wolf on its kill, but when my horse stopped I saw it sprinting across the alplands. I watched the wolf run across the snow and disappear in the high rocks. The wind had carried our scent and the wolf needed no further warning. Not once did it slow down or look back.

In the trail ahead a swath of red snow and drag marks angled down from above. I dismounted and followed the blood trail. In the willows I found the remains of a ewe sheep at the center of a packed circle of snow. Only the bloodied skull and forequarters were left. I backtracked a quarter-mile uphill to find where the wolf had surprised a small band of ewes and lambs. Coming fast from behind a concealing pile of rock, he'd charged downhill, making contact with the ewe forty yards from his hiding place. Blood splatters marked the spot, and the snow showed where she had fallen. Crimson stains told how the ewe had gotten to her feet and started to run, her entrails dragging in the snow. She came to ground for the last time on the slope just above where the carcass now lay. The wolf had pulled her downhill into the willows. In the eight hours or so since then, the wolf had gorged on forty pounds of meat.

V

When I first came north, old-timers advised that if I wanted to learn the ways of wolves, their most intimate ways, I should study with a trapper. All questions of motivation aside, to be successful a trapper *must* know the creatures he hunts.

My first close look at a wolf came when I examined a dead one. Four dead wolves, in fact. I'd flown into the Alaska Range to a cabin snugged in the timber at the head of a large river. On the way in the young pilot, who later would demonstrate his inability with a dramatic string of aerial mis-adventures, hollered over his shoulder: "Wolf on the river." I craned to see as he put the plane in a gut-wrenching turn. There, off the wingtip, a wolf stood stiff in midstride, staring back at us. We circled time and again. The wolf never moved.

"Young and dumb . . . and lucky," the pilot shouted when we had leveled out again and were headed upriver. "An old wolf would take off at the first sound of an engine. Hutch'd see to that" — Hutch being a Fairbanks-based aerial wolf hunter well known in the country for his mastery of hands-off flying while shooting wolves. Piles of frozen wolves, part of an annual kill estimated some years at eighty to one hundred, sometimes filled his yard. "For the good of the big game," he'd say. There were others around the state like him.

Soon our single-engine Citabria was gliding to a stop on the hard-packed snow strip in front of Jim Smith's cabin. His brother-in-law met us; Smith was gone and wouldn't be back that day. White smoke puffed straight up from the cabin's stovepipe into the sun-bright sky. A thermome-ter nailed to a tree stood at minus twenty. The frame cabin had a wall tent for an entryway. Snow was banked to wall height on all sides. "Keeps the heat in better," we were told. A walkway shoveled out of the snow led down into the tent. I ducked through the drawn-back door and dodged two wolf carcasses hanging from the tent ridgepole. They were stunning in size, their tails curled against the tent top, and their shoulders and heads folded against the ground, frozen stiffer than taxidermy.

Inside the small cabin another wolf, not so big as the others but still impressive, hung thawing by the tin stove. A fresh-skinned pelt hung by the nose from a nail driven into a purlin. This white one seemed to dwarf all the others. I held a pocket tape against the skin. From tip of tail to tip of nose, it measured eighty-eight inches.

We were told that Smith once had a scale in camp and weighed each wolf he caught. The largest weighed 135 pounds.

Tea had a distinctive flavor in that aromatic little cabin, and we didn't linger too long, a cooling airplane engine our excuse. Back in the Citabria, we roared off for Fairbanks. The pilot said that Smith, like the wolves he pursued, was unpredictable. He called Smith a hard worker, a tough woodsman-trapper. Once Smith had run out of tobacco and snowshoed over a mountain pass to reach town to buy cigarettes. The pilot had followed Smith's beeline trail over the mountains and found him headed back. In the dead of winter, Smith had snowshoed seventy miles for cigarettes.

A year passed before I met this storied man. Everybody had a Smith tale; every old mountain cabin had some comment of Smith's penciled on the wall, usually just the date and his catch or kill. I found him to be friendly and loquacious. He did not match some of the stories. He was a slight, bearded man, about five-eight, but plainly possessed of an endurance and strength usually found in much bigger men.

Smith indeed was an indefatigable worker and outdoorsman, one of those types who seem to live off coffee and cigarettes, yet run everyone else into the ground. He preferred being in the mountains, trapping, to living in town. I could easily picture him as one of the early mountain men of the American high plains.

He pursued fur with almost driven energy, and he caught a lot of it. A fur buyer once remarked that Smith caught more fur than most other trappers because "he works so damn hard."

One March I trucked him and his gear to Delta. There we unloaded his twin-tracked Alpine snowmachine, folding sled, and a canoe. Into the sled he put a bag of traps, some snares, coils of wire, a rifle, bedroll, an axe, cans of gasoline, and a wood crate containing ammunition, coffee, cookies, a cake, and fried chicken. He tied the canoe on top. After traveling many miles he would leave the canoe on the river and then go in pursuit of lynx— *link*, he called them. Lynx were traveling in the mating ritual, which made them easier to trap, and their fur was at a premium price. I picked him up two weeks later seventy-five miles or more across the Tanana Flats at Clear. He had twenty-one skins.

He amazed me with his limited, though specific, knowledge of animals. Whereas my knowledge came from formal training, reading, and some field experience, his came from personal observation. I admired that.

Smith did know wolves. Old-time trappers like Oscar Vogel and Elmer Simco, men who trapped on snowshoes and with dogteams, would speak with pride of catching nine wolves a season. Few other trappers could top them. For many seasons, employing the latest and best snow machines that money could buy, Smith could do no better. But one winter, the winter before the aerial wolf hunts were reinstated over the Tanana Flats, and a testament to wolf numbers then, Smith caught twenty-one wolves.

On his trapline south of the Tanana River, I saw how Smith set snares and traps, made baits and lures. I saw, too, the way the wolves, unlike the lynx, avoided them. Once we came on the track of five wolves that veered from the timber to follow the machine-packed trail. Smith stopped the Alpine at the single file of tracks. "Two adults and three pups," he said. Excitement glittered in his eyes. "Wolf set ahead."

I jumped back on the sled runners and we took off with a lurch. A half-mile down the trail we drove into the perimeter of a thin stand of black spruce and stopped. Smith cut the engine and shuffled forward in his black, quilted snowsuit to bend down over a spot in the trail. The wolf tracks stopped there. Smith described how they'd all looked down the trail when the leader sensed danger. The trap trail cut straight through the timber, but the wolf tracks angled away, circling through the unbroken snow around the thicket. I followed the loop to the far side of the timber, where the wolves regained the snow-machine trail. Here the tracks indicated that the wolves had looked back down the trail before continuing. I walked back thirty yards to where Smith bent over a spot in the snow.

"Can you see anything?" he asked. I saw nothing amiss but knew that a trap must be hidden there. He took a stick and plunged it into the snow. With a wicked snap the toothed jaws lunged into view. The wolves, ninety feet away, had sensed danger in the trail and avoided it, scribing a half-circle around the spot. Smith said they'd *smelled* the buried, frozen steel.

All that morning we found those half-circles where the wolves had come on other traps. They also avoided other spruce copses that *looked* like trap sites.

The wolves weren't always that smart or lucky. The pelts hanging in Smith's cabin and the stiff carcasses outside evidenced his skills.

It wasn't until I saw a trapped wolf for the first time that I experienced these animals' most startling trait—their eyes. Smith had told me that wolves usually don't fight the trap when the man comes near but instead crouch low and still. Yet I was ill-prepared when one day we came on a hunched, motionless shape caught in a trap. I thought at first it was another frozen kill. It wasn't. A black wolf, its forepaw mangled in a #114 double-spring Newhouse, waited by the side of a wolf-killed moose that Smith had ambushed. Unlike foxes and lynx, which twist and jump and try to escape, the wolf never moved as Smith walked up.

The look in those eyes. Unwavering eyes. Full of sadness, tinged with warning. The kind of look a truly superior person might give to thugs that have just savaged him, his flesh broken and battered but the spirit unbowed. The stare seemed to bore in, yet as Smith and I separated, I saw that it wasn't *us* the wolf looked at, but Smith, the man with the lethal little Colt Woodsman in his hand. How could it know? Smith raised the pistol but I said wait. Muttering, he lowered the gun. I walked in a slow circle around the wolf yet it never looked back; its eyes were pinned on Smith. When I reached his side, Smith raised the pistol and fired. The wolf jumped, thrashed, and fell unmoving to the ground, a bullet in the brain. Smith walked up and nudged the carcass with his foot. He placed the gun in his pocket and bent to undo the trap.

A few weeks later I was on his line again but riding the sled behind his trapping partner, Bill. This wolf, a white one, behaved as the other had, unmoving, hunkering close to the snow. Around the wolf a circle twelve feet in diameter had been packed hard, a clue to her struggles. Only the eyes moved, flickering from one to the other of us, but *what* eyes. Not brown like most wolves, but blue. *Light blue.* Bill saw it, too. "Look," is all he said. I wondered. No . . . no . . . this was no dog. No dog ever looked like this: the long legs, the big feet, the peculiar head. This was most certainly a wolf. Yet the only animals I'd ever seen with eyes of ice blue were sled dogs called Siberian huskies. Some of them had one brown and one blue eye. Others had these very same light blue eyes—eyes always a little disconcerting. Could it be that somewhere on a dark winter's night, at some remote community, a bitch wolf in lust's grasp had bred with a husky dog, returning to the bush to whelp her crossbred pups?

The look in her eyes. Whereas the black wolf had merely watched, these almost-human eyes all but *spoke.* I've killed a lot of animals for meat and horns, first on a ranch, then in the woods, feeling mixed pride and remorse at each animal's passing, but when Bill raised the pistol, I had to turn and walk away.

With Smith I saw where wolves had chased caribou, stalking, then pursuing them in the same way the black wolf on Dick Creek had caught the sheep. Rarely would the wolves make a kill. Sometimes they would eat most every scrap of meat, other times they'd eat very little. Smith said he'd once found a cow moose that the wolves had killed yet never returned to. Together we found where wolves had killed a mature bull moose. This wasn't an old, sick, or infirm animal but a healthy adult. The snow where the moose died was ankle deep, neither hindrance to moose nor advantage for wolves. Though it was early January, the bull still carried a heavy rack. I took Smith's axe and with a blow cracked a femur. The marrow was rich and good: the moose had not been starving. We saw no sign of deformation or disease, yet there, in a shelter of black spruce and birch, the bull died, pulled down after an epic struggle with seven large wolves. The nose flesh and cartilage, guts, and hams were eaten; the remainder of the moose was untouched. Smith set his traps by the carcass and placed snares in the approaches.

No wolf ever died there.

Over the three winters that I visited Smith's line, our friendship, always uncomfortable at best, began to erode. The last time, we went into the foothills below Mystic Creek. In the bottoms the snow was deep and the creek ice solid. Smith motored right along; I rode the sled runners. Just as the trail began rising to the pass, I saw four wolves running the ridgeline above us. I yelled myself hoarse until finally Smith heard me above the growl of the Alpine and stopped to look where I pointed.

"Get off," he yelled, leaping back to unhook the sled. He jerked his rifle from the frozen scabbard, slung it over his shoulder, and roared uphill after the wolves, now gone from view. Smith drove wildly, abandoning all the caution with which he usually traveled, jolting and slamming without pause over the rough, high ground. He soon zipped over the summit.

The engine roar died and I was alone in the silence. In thirty minutes he drove back and without comment hooked up the sled. "Hop on," he said. We started back up, retracing his path but driving slow, avoiding the worst bumps and hummocks. At the top he stopped the machine. He told me that he'd cut the engine here to look and listen. Then he'd palmed the 6mm to follow the wolf tracks on foot.

"Come on, I want to show you something." I followed. We walked along in his track and soon came to the wolf tracks. Smith's trail went parallel, across the tundra to the end of the tracks. I saw where Smith had stopped and turned around. I could see, too, where the wolves had run four abreast, flanking out from singlefile. Then the tracks simply vanished. The trail of the wolves' lengthening stride led to a spot . . . and stopped.

Though we walked in ever-widening circles, we failed to pick up the trail again. Sweeps with the 7X glasses showed scattered bands of caribou but no wolves. Perhaps the wind had come up suddenly and hidden the tracks. Perhaps. Yet in that moment, in that calm, quiet air, looking down at the tracks, like those made by ptarmigan taking to wing, I just had to look up.

VI

Jim Smith was a good trapper. He did not set his traps and leave them untended; he checked them often. I once asked him why he trapped. He said he lived in the woods "to get some peace." I never asked him what he felt about the animals he caught. I cannot even guess. I do know he had a special connection to wolves.

Some trappers are drawn by the life-style. They find satisfaction in learning the ways of animals while on the trail in winter, coping with the cold and isolation, having the whole world seemingly to themselves. Others trap of necessity. Employment in the bush is unreliable, seasonal at best, and the cost of living high. If it weren't for the money *and* the tie to tradition that trapping provides, many more villagers would be on the government dole.

Animal rights activists not only deplore the killing of animals for their fur but also bitterly oppose the use of leghold traps, which they see as barbaric instruments. Torturing animals for money, they say, is cruel and inhumane. Trappers reject these claims, saying trapping is good wildlife management. Trapping *is* a goal-oriented life-style. No one traps solely for the money. Throughout history, the relationship between the trapper and the fur buyer has been so one-sided that some trappers seem shocked if they *do* make a profit.

I knew an old trapper who worked a drainage on the far side of Cook Inlet for the skins of beaver, mink, fox, and otter. He was among the best. He farmed his area, never overtrapped. He took only a fixed number of beaver each year. With his selective trapping, the beaver population in the area expanded despite his annual catch. But though he always brought to town a great pile of furs, he always went home broke. He was broke because he was perennially cheated by a particular fur buyer. Most buyers try to shave the average in their favor but still offer a fair price. This buyer was different. He was dishonest.

The trapper never caught on. He would take his fur to the buyer and proudly display a winter's work. The buyer would carefully examine each pelt. He'd run his hand inside to check the skin and blow against the guard hairs to check the underfur. He would always praise the quality of the fur and the careful handling. Then he'd say in a sad voice that it certainly was too bad that these skins—fox, beaver, otter, whatever the trapper had—were not at all in demand and not bringing good prices. To back up his statement, he would disappear into the back room and come out with a printed memo form from one of the big fur houses on the coast. On it would be a hand-written note:

Dear ——,

Stop buying fox [or beaver, or otter, or mink]. The market price has dropped out.

Yours truly,

——

That was sufficient for my friend. He'd sell all his fur for next to nothing, happy to get what he could for it.

A few years after both the buyer and my friend had died, I learned that a local printer, at the fur buyer's order, had printed up a big batch of memo forms with company letterhead. He did not know what they would be used for. All those years the fur buyer had been writing his own memos on those forms to swindle the trappers.

I often thought of my friend and others like him out in the wild, risking life and limb in numbing cold, while that buyer sat back in comfort all winter, just waiting to make the kill.

Some trappers did get back at a few of the shady buyers. One man told me how he outsmarted a buyer whom he thought totally unfair. The trapper had taken in a batch of prime marten pelts, carefully and professionally handled. The buyer had offered three dollars apiece. The outraged trapper also was told that the price would be five times higher if the pelts were more closely "matched" in color. He stewed over this all summer and through the next trapping season. Finally he came up with a plan. While on the trapline he experimented with hair dyes and coloring. After much trial, he came up with a blend that he called Prime Dark Marten.

That spring, needless to say, the trapper got the top price for the carefully selected and matched dark marten he brought to the buyer. The scheme could only work once, however. The trapper's Prime Dark Marten coloring washed out in tanning. Both parties kept the whole thing quiet.

VII

Some Native trappers and hunters have a great respect for, if not fear of, wolves. Although in North America only a few attacks on humans have been documented, mostly by rabid animals, the Natives' perception is that wolves do kill people. Trappers and hunters have disappeared, and some village elders tell of friends or relatives lost to wolves. Robert Stephenson, a wolf researcher, has a picture of a human skull found inside a wolf den. No one knows how the skull came to be there. Stephenson suspects that it was scavenged from an above-ground burial site, but given the lack of evidence, he does not rule out direct predation.

VIII

Aerial wolf killing: for the last quarter-century no subject has stirred more controversy in wildlife circles in Alaska than this emotional issue. Until the early seventies anyone who could get an airplane and a hunting license could legally fly out and shoot wolves from the air. Many did just that.

Some hunted wolves to promote big game populations, in the belief that predator control was good game management; others hunted wolves for sport. The large majority of those who tried, for whatever motive, had little success. Flying slow and low to the ground while attempting to shoot at a running, dodging target proved dangerous. Planes were wrecked and human lives lost. Only a handful of pilots, maybe ten or twenty, actually mastered aerial wolfing. A few top wolfers took along shooters, but some of these men not only flew their planes but did the shooting as well. A good wolfer could bring in a hundred wolves a year. In 1972 the State of Alaska outlawed aerial wolfing for sport and commercial purposes, but the practice persisted as Alaska Department of Fish and Game workers, or their permitees, continued reduction programs.

I learned to fly in 1970. A lot of my friends were pilots. Some of them were wolfers, and I listened to their tales with interest. It sounded dangerous. I could not imagine being able to fly a Piper Cub and at the same time accurately fire a shotgun out the open window. I had a hard enough time getting a Cub to do what I wanted using both hands.

When an acquaintance—I'll call him Leon—asked me to go along on a wolf shoot, I agreed. He was widely known as one of the top bush pilots in the country, and a skilled wolfer. Here was the chance to experience, with what I hoped was minimal risk, this controversial business.

Leon briefed me on his technique. We'd wait until after a fresh snow, to make tracking easier, then we'd follow wolf tracks to the wolves. Once over the pack, Leon would open the door—Super Cub doors are hinged at top and bottom—and descend on the wolves in slow flight. Just before closing to within shotgun range, he'd put the plane in a slip to offer a broad field of fire. He'd then empty the six-shot automatic into the wolves.

Sounded simple enough, but the danger was obvious. For this to work, Leon would have to have both hands free to fire the shotgun. (He never let greenhorns like me shoot from his plane.) He would pilot the plane by clutching the control stick between his knees. At this critical moment in a critical maneuver, his concentration would be diverted from the controls and instruments. Less than one hundred feet above the ground, we would be in a flaps-down slip so that stray shot or poor timing would not sever a strut or damage a propeller. Reverse-aileron stall, a hazard of such flying, could turn into a lethal spin. Other unpleasantries awaited a judgment error, a mechanical failure, a miscalculation, or a moment's indecision.

On a clear subzero morning, following a heavy snowfall, we took off from Birchwood Airport. As the platitude goes, I could tell by the way Leon taxied the plane that he was an expert. A light plane on skiis— obviously it has no brakes—isn't easy to maneuver on the ground, but Leon weaved among the parked planes and out onto the strip with no difficulty. Once we were over the inlet, I relaxed. Leon was no hot dog. Every move was precise, coordinated, and smooth. I sat back for a long day's ride.

We flew across Knik Arm, down the west side of Cook Inlet and through Merrill Pass. The fresh snow on the mountains was bathed in bright sunlight. Even at two thousand feet I think we could have seen tracks below. The plane was anything but warm, and the engine noise so loud that conversation was impossible. Dressed in overpants, snowboots, and heavy parka, I sat on a canvas seat with survival gear jammed in around me. I held a loaded shotgun upright between my knees. My job would be to hand it forward without blowing a hole in the plane.

On the west side of the Alaska Range we dropped to nine hundred feet and began searching drainages for tracks. Even from that altitude Leon could easily distinguish a wolf track. Often I'd point out tracks only to have them identified as moose or caribou. A couple of hours into the flight, I began to discover one of the most important traits required of a successful aerial wolfer, a large bladder.

We landed at Farewell Station for lunch—and a pit stop—at the flight service station. We'd crossed the west side of the range from Merrill to Farewell and seen nary a wolf or track. All the talk about huge packs ravaging the game seemed just that, talk.

After lunch we flew through Rainy Pass, over Ptarmigan Valley, down the Happy River, and out over the Yentna River Valley. A little after dark we were back in Anchorage.

The next day we flew the same route, in the same pattern. Just south of Farewell, I was looking out the right side when suddenly the plane banked left. "Tracks," Leon shouted over his shoulder. Below, a heavy single-file trail wound through a black spruce scrub that stretched for miles. To me the trails looked no different than others we'd seen, but Leon said these were made by wolves.

As we S-turned along the meandering track, I began to feel the excitement. Leon was alert, bolt upright in the seat. We flew for twenty minutes without seeing the wolves. Soon the trail led into the dense white spruce and cottonwood along the Big River. We zipped out over the river, turned east, then west, but the trail never broke from the timber.

After circling for a while, time enough to check gas gauges, oil pressure, and judge distant clouds and sunlight, we decided not to continue the chase. Leon turned toward Farewell, and home.

The third day started the same but ended in a way I won't forget. In Merrill Pass we flew over wolf tracks leading down from a mountain slope. The wolves were heading west. Leon stayed high until we were through the narrow part of the pass, then let down to within five hundred feet of the ground. Out each side the mountains rose above us. The air was calm and cold. In summer there would have been turbulence.

Where the valley widened we came on the wolves. I felt the carb heat come on, the power cut back, and saw Leon notch in full flaps. We were in a rapid descent. In another moment the window came up and I was engulfed in a blast of frigid air. Leon was yelling. After a blank moment, I understood and handed up the gun, sticking the barrel out the window. I looked over Leon's shoulder and saw four wolves running a quarter mile ahead of us. Beyond them timberline promised safety. Even in slow flight we rapidly gained on the wolves. Two obviously had been shot at before. They cut away from us at almost right angles in a zigzagging run.

I felt the plane twist into a slip. I saw the gun come up, and the wolf running directly ahead. A deafening blast. Then two more shots. The ground was coming up fast. Quickly the plane slewed into level flight, the power came full on, and we were in a sharp turn. I could see none of the animals, only white snow frightfully close below. We came out of the bank and to the right there was another wolf, a darker one. The power went, the plane slipped, then three quick shots. This time I saw the wolf stumble, pitch, and roll. The power came on and we leveled out but now directly ahead was a line of sixty-foot spruce. We flew straight at the trees. In seconds we would hit them. My mind was shouting *climb!* We hadn't yet enough airspeed to make such a climb, but *climb!* Leon had to hold full power and wait until the last second for all the airspeed he could muster. Too abrupt a control movement and we'd go down. At what seemed beyond the last moment, Leon pulled back on the stick and we shot up over the trees.

We continued to climb, then leveled out into a shallow turn. Leon closed the window. I'd forgotten the wind and cold. Every nerve vibrated.

"Two got into the timber, but I got the others," he yelled back. Soon we were taxiing on the snow and up to the first wolf. In the distance lay the darker one. I was glad to get out of the plane.

After wrapping an insulated cover over the cowling to hold in engine heat, Leon joined me where I stood looking down at the wolf. The snow was white. There was no blood there or on the wolf. The tiny buckshot holes had not bled past the skin. It was strange to stand there looking down at the shape. It was not much different than looking down at a stray dog that you see dead by the side of the road.

"Gave us a good run for our money," he said, poking the wolf with his foot. "Hides aren't worth much this year but this one won't kill any more sheep." For him that was what it was all about.

Over the years I've thought a lot about that trip. Even before going, I knew wolfing was not for me. Some people called it hunting, but *hunting* it was not. It was something totally different. Even the response to death was different. I've never felt so removed from an animal's passing as I did when looking down at that dead wolf.

A few winters later I would compare these emotions and thoughts with those I experienced on the trapline. I knew Smith felt strongly about the animals he killed. He was an opponent of aerial wolf hunting. He cared about wolves.

"It's one thing to face an animal on the ground and kill it," he once said, "another thing to shoot it from the air." What he didn't have to say was that on the ground, a person has to look the animal in the eye and pull the trigger. From the air the value of an animal is greatly diminished. It becomes something seen rather than experienced, a target rather than a living creature. "If the populations are healthy, I don't have any problem with trapping or shooting an animal," Jerre Wills, a trapper and homesteader once told me, "but it's hard to walk up and look a trapped wolf in the eye and see that intelligence burning there. You just can't miss it, or shrug it off. I always feel bad."

Often I draw the parallel between killing wolves and warfare. When I served in the Army, I met many combat veterans. The grunts that slogged the jungle and confronted the enemy all seemed to bear heavy burdens. They had to look the enemy in the eye and kill or be killed. Scars were deep. Some of the bomber pilots, who from thirty-five thousand feet rained death and immense destruction on the land below, did not appear to bear the same burdens. Though I can't say such a man does not exist, I have never met an aerial wolf hunter who displayed much empathy for the wolf.

IX

In Alaska, whenever large-mammal populations decline, wolves get the blame. A few studies indicate that wolves under certain circumstances can reduce moose populations. Many other studies indicate that predation can become a devastating influence only after some other factor, such as harsh weather, disease, overhunting, or a combination, has come into play.

In the early seventies one wildlife scientist working in Interior Alaska formulated the controversial hypothesis that snowshoe hares might have been one important factor in the decline of moose populations in the Tanana Valley near Fairbanks. His theory is a classic example of the interplay within the natural world.

Snowshoe hares are remarkably fecund, having as many as three litters per summer with an average of ten young per litter (and a high of eighteen per litter). This fecundity allows the species to increase its numbers dramatically every eight to eleven years. In Alberta, scientists found that before a major die-off, hares peaked at 3,000 to 5,900 per square mile. Interior Alaskan populations in the 1970s peaked at 1,600 to 1,900 hares per square mile. Even the most casual observer cannot fail to note this remarkable explosion. Hares, and their tracks and sign, are everywhere.

During the upswing in the hare cycle, predator populations boom. Corresponding increases in numbers of lynx, fox, coyote, and great horned owls are well-documented. Large hare populations are also a prey source for denning wolves.

Turn-of-the-century naturalists postulated that hare populations declined because of disease and predation, but in the 1970s, scientists in

Alaska and Canada concluded that it appeared to be not predation that caused the sudden crash in hare populations but rather nutrition. Hares have the capability of eating themselves out of house and home—literally. Although it was true that predators had increased and expanded because of the abundance of hares, only after the hares began to die off from starvation did predation become a dominant mortality factor on the declining populations. The controversial aspect of the hypothesis stated that in deep-snow years, as overpopulation forced hares to emigrate from prime habitat, they moved into moose winter range and competed for a limited food supply. In some instances, hares outcompeted the moose and removed all of the winter browse available to both species.

These studies came at a time when moose populations in Interior Alaska were in a steady decline, due in part to wolf predation, severe winter weather, and some overhunting. From a high of six thousand in 1970, moose populations in the Tanana Valley fell to about three thousand in 1975. Calf survival rates hit record lows.

The severe winter of 1970–71 coincided with the prepeak year in the hare cycle. The record snowfall of that winter limited moose movement and reduced available forage, thus precipitating an overwinter mortality rate that some biologists pegged as high as fifty percent. The study hypothesized that food competition with hares further limited browse availability, which resulted in a greater moose mortality than would have been the case with low hare populations. For the human populations bordering the Tanana Valley, who prized moose meat as a staple, the decline was a disaster.

The abundant prey base of ubiquitous hares and starving moose probably allowed wolves to increase rapidly in numbers. Then, in 1974, hare populations in the Tanana Valley crashed, going from superabundance one year to virtual nonexistence the next. With the demise of the snowshoe hare populations, wolves turned increasingly to moose and caribou as prey. In 1976, in the face of mounting controversy, aerial wolf control began again over the Tanana Valley.

X

Downriver a boiling wall of black clouds filled the canyon of the Koyukuk while thunder boomed across the peaks. The promise of rain perfumed the hard wind. I'd been on a long journey to the North Slope, and the last thing I wanted was to be caught out in a cloudburst. I'd hoped to make camp before nightfall, but now I turned downhill toward the river thickets that promised shelter for my small tent.

A well-used trail led along a sparsely forested ridge that bisected the muskeg. I hurried down it toward the river. I was busy watching my feet and failed to see the movement until I was nearly on top of it. I saw the fur ball running just ahead of me as it cut off the trail and disappeared in the brush. *Grizzly cub!* Reflexively I backed up a step. No! *Cross fox.* I stopped, my heart hammering. *That's no bear, no fox.* The realization came in slow motion. *Wolf pup.* The first in the wild I'd seen. I shrugged out of my pack and started after the wolf. I broke through the line of brush and looked out over an expanse of muskeg with hardly enough cover to hide a lemming. Wondering if the wolf family had been fragmented and this was a lost pup, I turned and continued through the brush toward the river. In this same way I'd once found a coyote pup far from its den.

The wind came in a continuous blast now, shaking the stunted black spruce and rattling the needles. I hurried on as the thunder seemed to break right overhead. All at once I was on the den and standing on the dirt mounds packed hard by the lolling bodies of wolves, young and old. There were gnawed bones and tufts of sheep hair, and the smell of scats and urine. For a moment I stood in the trees and stared, then almost as if my feet burned I jumped away from the yawning holes and headed downhill.

On the flat I looked back up at the den. The wolves had dug at the end of the ridge, where it dropped off sharply to the river. Although protected by the thin timber, the den commanded the valley. Sensing movement behind me, I whirled in time to see four pups running away from the den and toward the heavy brush that lined the riverbank. One tumbled and fell head over tail, but was up and running in a moment, hardly missing a stride. The pups varied in color from that of a cross fox to the deep black of a bear. They looked as fat and wide as they were long, their short stubby tails a comical counterpoint to their bulk.

Surprised to see the pups running away from the den, I decided to return to my pack and allow the wolves to seek the protection of their den. Before I could turn away, and just beyond where the pups had run into the brush, a large white wolf appeared. Perhaps it had called the pups and I had not heard it over the storm. But now it was barking at me. Barking just like a dog. A harsh, unrelenting cadence. The anxiety was unmistakable.

I felt no fear but rather an intense disquiet. Although this was the first den I'd ever discovered, I backed away, wanting to get as far from it in as short a time as possible. The barking nagged me as I hurried uphill and passed the den. In fact, the wolf was following me and so indeed the sound did not diminish. I stopped, and on an impulse, I howled. The barking stopped and the wolf howled its answer. A strange relief washed over me as I replied in kind. And so it was that I continued to talk to the wolf as I hurried away to my pack.

The trees shook in the gale, the howling finally drowned out by the tumult and thunder. Shouldering my pack, I hurried south and into the face of the storm. In minutes, before I could reach shelter, the cloudburst struck.

XI

Why wolves stir strong emotions within us, I'm not sure. Lots of reasons, no doubt, though none are perfectly clear. Perhaps it's because the wolf is so close to us, harkening back to days when man and wolf lived closer together, competing and later cooperating in the hunt for meat. Then again, more simply, it might just be that the wolf is so doglike — man's best friend — as to arouse, in many people at least, our empathy and compassion. Most people, whether they own one or not, like dogs. We like their loyalty, their companionship, their "love" (though bought at the price of food), and their subdued ferocity, when needed to protect us. To some people, for ill-defined reasons, wolves pose a threat far beyond that of marauders of game and livestock.

There is no denying that wolves in Alaska, especially during territorial days when the federal government managed the wildlife, have been victimized by almost every kind of killing device. Poison, traps, snares, set-guns, wing-mounted automatic weapons, and booby traps of every type. Legend has it that Inuit* would freeze the butts of razor-edged knives in the snow and smear the blades with tallow. A wolf finding the knife would lick at the blade, cut its tongue, then lap furiously at the taste of fresh blood. Death would follow. The Inuit also hid sharpened baleen slivers, bent double and tied with rawhide, inside bait balls. The wolf (or fox) would gulp the bait;

---

*Inuit, meaning "the people," is the Natives' own appellation for themselves. Eskimo, "eaters of raw meat," is an Indian name for the Inuit — and a word I prefer not to use.

when the rawhide had dissolved in the stomach acid, the baleen stabbed the animal from the inside.

Government predator control men refined that technique by using cyanide guns, called getters. The unsuspecting animal would bite the bait and shoot itself in the mouth with a lethal dose of cyanide. Some of the country, especially the Nelchina Basin, was laced with getters.

Years after the damn things were outlawed, a young man working for the Geodetic Survey was walking a ridgeline in the Fortymile country. He kicked what he thought was an odd-shaped mushroom. The cyanide gun went off, a fragment nearly tearing his little finger from his hand. A shot in the face would have killed him. The poison worked fast, but he survived, though to this day he does not have complete use of his hand. How old was the device? Some thought twenty years. But more probably some fool had placed it the winter before.

Though wolves were the main target, entire regions were stripped of animals in the name of wolf control. Bait stations—dead caribou or moose surrounded with poison baits—were placed at random throughout selected parts of the country. Everything that fed there died. Magpies, ravens, eagles, gray jays, shrews, voles, wolves, foxes, lynx, mink, marten, black bears, and grizzlies fell victim. Anything that ate meat. The late Don Sheldon showed me a picture of a pile—yes, a *pile*—of dead grizzlies at a bait station.

Perhaps the most stunning example of cruelty toward a living creature that I have ever heard of was told to me by a man I met at Lake Louise Lodge back in 1968. The man was introduced as the "best dang wolf trapper in the Nelchina." Not having much experience with wolves or wolf trappers, I paid uncommon attention to what he said.

The main secret to wolf trapping, he said, was to "keep it simple." Forget all about traps and snares, baits and lures, snowshoes and dogteams. All one really needed, he said, was halibut hooks, aircraft cable, and bait. Using a length of cable he dangled a baited hook from a stout tree limb so that the baited hook hung about five feet above the ground. A wolf would jump up to take the bait, the arc of its leap setting the hook. The best part, I was told, was that the wolf would be frozen, dangling in midair; the pelt, *if you wanted it*, would be safe from shrews, voles, and other rodents.

He was anything but a trapper.

Perhaps the more blatant excesses of wolf control are behind us, yet wolves are still killed from the air. A constant firestorm of controversy

surrounds aerial wolf hunting. On the one hand are activists insisting that
no wolves be killed; on the other are those who would control wolves to
benefit moose, caribou, deer, and sheep populations. It would appear to be
a confrontation that pits hunter against nonhunter. But it isn't that simple.

Many hunters support aerial wolf hunts, many do not. One of the
most vociferous opponents of aerial wolf hunting is a hunting guide, a
former military officer. One of the strongest proponents of aerial hunting is
a nonhunter, a nationally recognized wildlife scientist. This biologist points
out that the wolf control program does not threaten the extinction or
extermination of wolves. Rather, the goal is to increase moose and caribou,
which eventually will also result in the increase of wolves. The goal is to
double moose numbers, and in eight or nine years, double wolf numbers.

No matter how clearly game managers state their case, the real issue
lives apart from statistics. Emotions run high, facts matter little. The use of
modern technology to control wolves does not enjoy wide support. (Ironically, naturalists who make up their minds not to kill appear to empathize
with the predators, the bears and wolves.) Aircraft, automatic or semiautomatic weaponry, and radio-tracking devices to find wolves are viewed by
many as the cruel and unethical employment of technology to persecute
animals. Aerial wolf control, even when carried out only by state em-
ployees, appears to contradict nationwide efforts to show that hunters
pursue their activity according to principles and rules of fair chase. For
game managers not to abide by similar rules in these management programs
can be confusing and contradictory, eliciting public skepticism that threat-
ens the very credibility of Alaska's Department of Fish and Game.

Aerial wolf control clearly is not hunting. Hunting, at the least, implies
giving the prey a chance. A wolf with a radio collar around its neck, tracked
by a helicopter guided by a radio receiver, and pursued by men armed with
semiautomatic weapons does not have a chance.

Trappers, even using snowmachines, cannot control wolf populations.
The country is too big and the wolves too smart. But add aircraft, poisons,
radio-tracking devices, sophisticated communications, all coupled with
growing human population and reduced habitat, and this advantage shifts
rapidly—no, *radically*—to man. Perhaps we already possess the ability to
eradicate wolves in Alaska, only the pressures against the use of poison and
aircraft have prevented it.

A greater, unchallenged threat to wolves, and all Alaska's wildlife,
meanwhile goes largely unnoticed. Politicians push hard for agricultural

development in Alaska. There is hardly a more unlikely place for farming and ranching in this hemisphere. Nevertheless, government projects have cleared tens of thousands of acres of prime wildlife habitat, turning it into poor-quality farmland. A red-meat industry is planned. Soon domestic cattle and sheep might graze public lands now solely the realm of wildlife. It isn't hard to imagine what will happen when wolves and bears begin to take a toll on livestock.

The rich grassland of Kodiak Island, the home of the giant brown bear, has already seen the classic confrontation between livestock interests and wildlife, a battle that historically has resulted in the elimination of native predators. Early Russian settlers on Kodiak lost cattle to brown bears. Not surprisingly, in the early sixties modern ranchers were demanding state help because bears seemed to be killing livestock in alarming numbers. In response, a Super Cub was specially outfitted with a roof-mounted automatic rifle and used to shoot brown bears from the air. Though bears were killed only on the ranches, the killing did not specifically target known cattle killers. It looked for a while as though Alaska was handling the situation in the time-worn way: when faced with a wildlife problem, eliminate the wildlife. The inescapable irony was that the federal government had established a refuge on Kodiak for the protection of brown bears and then issued grazing leases on the north end of the island adjacent to the refuge. Conflict was inevitable.

Hunters and wildlife enthusiasts were outraged. Jim Rearden, writing in the August 1964 issue of *Outdoor Life* magazine, blew the whistle. The resulting national pressure brought an end to the aerial killing of brown bears.

Alaska is one of the few places in the world with viable, largely intact populations of grizzlies and wolves. Only with foresight, innovation, and creative conservation will these great predators avoid the fate of their brethren in the Lower Forty-Eight.

XII

Years ago I spent a winter in a small log cabin that I built for Will and Lurue Troyer on the Juneau Lake Trail near Cooper Landing. One night there lingers in my memory.

It was late winter, snowing and warm. After a full day of gathering firewood, I went to bed early and slept well until about two A.M. The howling of wolves woke me—a howling louder and more vibrant than any I'd ever heard. In the darkness I felt the wolves moving around me. I felt a part of the pack.

Two o'clock in the morning is not a good time for me. I don't like it when the world is pitch dark. I admit to feelings of fear, surprise, confusion. It took me a long time to realize that I was in my sleeping bag and the wolves were outside the cabin. Just *feet* from the window.

How long the wolves howled I don't know. All I do know is that I laid there stiff and unmoving, afraid to make any sound that would break the spell.

The howling stopped. There was no crescendo, no dramatic withering wail. Just sudden silence. The silence of a quiet, dark night. I took a deep breath, sat up. Though I waited a long time, I heard nothing more.

The next morning I was up early and outside. The proof was there. *It had been no dream.* Two wolves had come down the trail and walked up to the cabin. Their tracks were fresh in the powder. Thirty feet from the front door they'd sat and howled.

That evening, just at dark, I went out on the porch to take the cool, night air. I'd forgotten the wolves but seeing where they had been, I remembered. I thought of how my friend Rollie stood outside his cabin every night and howled like a wolf to see if any would answer. I'd always snickered at his phony howling, but I thought now I'd try . . . no, that's foolish. I went back inside.

Still the idea haunted me, and in a few minutes I was back on the porch. I took a deep breath and howled. It seemed too high-pitched, phonier even than Rollie's. Surely, no wolf would be fooled. In disgust I turned to go in when to my utter astonishment, from the ridge up the trail, the wolves returned my howl. I waited, then howled again.

They answered. Closer. After a long pause I tried again and directly came the response, but this time from just below the cabin. I strained to see the wolves, half-expecting the shapes to come bounding through the timber. Long moments passed in silence. I howled again but at once knew it was a mistake. At this distance, the wolves would not be conned. I shivered on the porch until full darkness, then went inside. The next day, I found their tracks a few yards below the outhouse. They had come very close.

I did not see or hear the wolves again, but a day later I heard that someone had seen two wolves running on the river ice below Troyer's cabin. The man grabbed his rifle and fired five shots at them. He missed.

FOUR

CARIBOU
Tundraland

I

On the crest of a low hill north of the old log roadhouse at Sourdough, just at dawn at nine-thirty, Nick slowed the Volkswagen to a stop on the left shoulder of the Richardson Highway, and we got out to look. After the nine-hour drive from Anchorage, it felt good to be finally in hunting country. The Nelchina Caribou Herd, sixty thousand animals, was reportedly crossing the road in this area. We sought winter meat.

The land sloped away from us to a timbered basin that rose in the west to a series of rolling hills, their domes hidden in the low cloud cover. Numerous frozen ponds, water courses, and muskeg swamps broke the stands of slender birch and thickets of stunted spruce. Tangles of alder and willow skirted the hills and choked the waterways where flocks of ptarmigan fed, undisturbed except by foxes. Caribou trails laced the snow, winding from the west, moving east, toward us.

The gray and white panorama whispered of caribou and of awesome cold that under clear skies could plunge to minus-forty and lower. The clouds that brought snow formed an insulating blanket that held in the earth's warmth. Now it was ten above, the warmest day in two weeks. The stillness, broken only by the squeak of snow underfoot, whispered excitement. I could hardly wait to push through the thickets, rifle in hand.

A white patrol sedan of the Alaska State Troopers, with blue hash mark and gold shield bright on the door, came around a bend and stopped next to us. The trooper, with a wary look for traffic, got out of the car.

"You can't park there," he said over the roof. "You must park on the correct side of the road."

"Okay," Nick replied. "We just stopped to look, we'll move on."

The trooper started to duck inside but Nick spoke again.

"Seen any caribou?"

"Sure. You've already driven by hundreds of the damn things. There's a big bunch just up ahead. Drive safely and stay on the right side of the road."

He slammed the door and drove off. He spoke as if tired of hunters and the same old questions. He probably thought caribou and caribou hunters were a nuisance.

We got back in the car and continued north.

"Did you hear that? *Hundreds of 'em.* We're finally here, Tom."

A few miles north, where the road sloped off the hills and onto the flats, we came to vehicles parked on the shoulder in a cloud of white

Lords of the Realm 2 cheat codes

exhaust. A woman sat waiting in one of the cars and waved a handful of knitting as we cruised by. The others were empty, their occupants nowhere in sight, but their engines were idling. A large number of caribou trails crossed the road. On the east side, boot tracks overtrod those of caribou.

We drove on but soon came to three more cars parked at the edge of the road where several deep trenches furrowed the berm. To the east we could see several figures bent over, steam rising about them as they worked to gralloch caribou.

We drove slower then, expecting at any minute to see caribou crossing the road. In the next five miles, except for two magpies that hopped away from a snowshoe hare crushed into the tarmac, we saw countless trails but no living creatures.

Tired of driving and eager to hunt, Nick turned off the highway and onto a side road that led west a half-mile to a small lake, where a number of cars and several snowmachines were parked next to two large tents. Just as we got out of the car, two snowmachines roared off across the lake. In a moment they were out of sight, but within a minute I heard the engines stop, then the sharp snap of gunfire.

I looked at Nick. He just shrugged and locked the car. We walked toward the lake in silence. The unplowed road, hard-packed from the passage of vehicles and snowmachines, skirted a low hill forested with spindly birch and spruce all but buried in deep, soft powder.

We walked under the overhanging branches to the first tent pitched at the dead end, a ten-man G.I. pyramid tent. White smoke puffed straight up from its stovepipe. A snowmachine, a Johnson Ski-Horse, lay on its side next to the tent. Beside it was a large, tarp-covered pile. I had almost walked by before I realized that the tarp protected a mound of gutted caribou. Legs and heads stained with blood jutted from beneath the tarp. Huge, cloven, hooves splayed out from stiffened legs. I began to count. Twenty, forty, sixty, eighty, eighty-four. *Eighty-four hooves.* Twenty-one caribou. A limit of three each for seven hunters.

Both disquieted and a little excited by the sight, I followed Nick to the lake. We passed still more dead caribou, some in the back of a pickup, a few on the ground, and one still tied with a rope to the back of a snowmachine. Down the lake we could see the two snowmachines, the drivers leaning over two caribou.

"It's getting late; shouldn't we try it here?" Nick asked in a whisper, as if in some holy place.

Before I could reply, an older man walked up. Despite the ragged parka and grimy snowpants, he was obviously a G.I.

"You fellows going to hunt?"

"We're going to give it a try," Nick said.

"Plenty caribou for everbody," he said with a heavy southern drawl. "Another day or two and we'll be hunted out and headin' home. We're stayin' at Sourdough and comin' here for the day. Bes' place around. You fellows have machines?"

"Nope. Hunting on foot," I said.

He looked a little surprised but wished us well as he walked away.

We went up the road toward the car to get our gear and guns. Behind us a snowmachine started up and roared off down the lake. Soon silence, followed by gunfire.

Back at the car I dressed in overpants and down parka. While we loaded our packs, Nick talked a streak. He had never hunted big game before, only small game in his native Vermont, and the dead caribou had him excited. I felt uncomfortable. I am never happy hunting around other people or when the outcome seems certain. I told myself that this was different. I was hunting not for sport but for the freezer.

We worked out a plan. I would cross the lake and hunt the west side while Nick worked the east side. We would meet at the south end. If either of us killed a caribou, the plan was to gut it and drag it out onto the lake. Later we'd both drag it back to the car. Nick wanted a limit; I wanted only one. Privately, I vowed that if Nick killed more than one caribou, I would not shoot anything because I knew that eventually I'd end up sharing his meat. Besides, how many caribou could be tied over the roof of a VW bug?

I waved to Nick and started across the lake. I stopped often, not so much because of the nearly knee-deep snow, but to watch the snowmachines coming and going. One came by dragging three caribou. On the half-mile walk to the far shore, I twice saw small groups of caribou break across the lake only to be turned back into the timber by the sudden roar of snowmachines.

It didn't take long to see what was happening. Men waited in the warmth of their vehicles until they saw caribou move onto the lake. Then they would start their snowmachines and race down to within rifle range of the caribou and start shooting.

The animals were beginning to learn. Just the sound of an engine starting was enough to send some caribou running for timber. As soon as the caribou turned back, the men would turn their machines around. There was no need to follow. There would be more. Always more. And more. Just wait.

I stopped to load my rifle before heading into the timber. I had the creepy feeling of loaded guns at my back. I planned to walk far enough into the woods to have at least minimal protection from errant bullets. I did not expect the snowmachiners to be either careful or expert shooters. Perhaps some of them even fired from *moving* machines. I shuddered at the thought. My enthusiasm for this hunt waned all the more.

In the timber my outlook began to change. The powder was thigh-deep in places. Big flakes started falling in feathery spirals. The gnarled black spruce, heavy with snow, muffled all sound but my own labored breathing. I could have been a hundred miles from the nearest road or human being. I had seldom seen a forest look so unreal. The misshapen timber, a result of the underlying permafrost, took even stranger form under the snow load that, without thaw or wind, had accumulated just as it had fallen. Green boughs showed only where caribou had brushed against them.

Caribou trails crisscrossed through the timber, and I pushed as quietly as possible from one trail to another, expecting momentarily to bump into a herd. Although I stayed well away from the lake, twice I heard muffled shots. Each seemed distant and not as disturbing as when I'd been in the open. I wondered about Nick. Had he killed a caribou? I hoped not, because I wanted to. Not just for the meat now but to show these people that a snowmachine wasn't needed. To prove it was possible to stalk among the caribou and take a life without bringing panic to the herd.

It was hard going in the timber and my view was limited. I thought about moving closer to the lake so that I could see more but prudently I stayed in the timber, hoping for a close shot.

I struggled around a thicket and came upon a dead caribou. It had fallen in its tracks, and judging by the trace of partly melted snow covering it, it had been dead only a few hours. Following the blood trail, I back-tracked just forty yards to the lake and found where it had been shot. A snowmachine had driven to the spot and the driver had dismounted. He couldn't have missed seeing the blood trail but instead of following the wounded animal, he had turned around and driven away.

I trudged back to the bloated caribou. I examined the brown and white fur, the short polished antlers, the delicate ears and face now stained with blood from the nostrils. I found a bullet wound in the cow's chest. The legs were stiff; the meat, despite the cold, was spoiled, cooked from within. I was shocked. This was a crime I could not understand.

Later I came upon two more badly bloated caribou—now food for foxes, ravens, and even perhaps wolves. Why hadn't the shooters followed these animals? Claimed the meat? I just couldn't get it straight. I grew angry. Later I would learn that in the excitement of encountering a group of animals, some shooters would fire into the herd, killing some animals outright, wounding others, seldom bothering to follow tracks to account for their shots. In some cases, in some places, for every one caribou killed and retrieved, perhaps another ran off wounded.

All joy was gone from the hunt. I vowed, again, to shoot at an animal only if a clear, killing shot was possible. And only in a place where, if the shot went bad, I could follow the animal with a good chance of soon finding it.

I struggled to the end of the lake without seeing a live caribou. The only living thing I saw was a raven beating slowly through the falling snow. Two miles from the car I waited for Nick at a point of land that jutted into the lake. Through the thickening snow I could see snowmachines crossing the far end of the lake. In fifteen minutes Nick came slogging through the timber.

"Did you get one?"

I shook my head.

"Damn. Heard shots. Hoped it was you. I saw some, though. Fell in deep snow and just as I got up three caribou came running from the lake. Tried to follow 'em but couldn't move fast enough. They went toward the highway."

For a long time we stood in silence watching the snow fall.

We talked things over and decided to hunt where we were. The snow was falling faster, blotting out the end of the lake. Perhaps the caribou would start moving now. I'd stay on the point, by the tallest spruce, while Nick moved back along the shore to another lookout. We'd try waiting for the caribou to come to us. If some did, we'd have to be careful about getting in the line of fire from down the lake, as well as watching our own firing backgrounds. I knew now why in Anchorage the caribou crossing on the Richardson was called the firing line.

I poked the snow from the lower branches of the big spruce and stomped out a place to sit. I took off my pack and got out my heavy parka to put on over my wool shirt. I folded the pack and sat on it, back to the tree. The few flakes that penetrated the branches to fall on my nylon parka slid to the ground, but the cereal-sized flakes soon covered my legs. The silence roared under the muffling cloak of snow. Again, for a moment, I had the happy feeling of being alone in a far distant place.

For over an hour the heavy snowfall muffled all sound. No snow-machines. No shooting. No ravens. No highway noise. Only the small sounds I made fidgeting against cold and immobility. The lake was a complete whiteout. I could not see either timbered shore.

Finally the snow began to lighten and I could see thirty yards, then forty, then one hundred, then halfway down the lake. Two caribou, a small bull followed by a cow, came out of the timber to my left. Although only eighty yards from them, I got to my feet without being seen. I raised my rifle, then lowered it, waiting for Nick to shoot. In the silence, the caribou grew bolder, began to trot. I could wait no longer—I had to shoot while the background was safe. I brought up my rifle, sighted on the bull's neck, and pulled the trigger. At the loud and vulgar roar the bull jumped forward, stumbled once, and fell kicking in the snow. I worked another cartridge into the chamber but did not shoot at the cow racing across the lake. In moments she'd crossed the lake and disappeared into the heavy timber.

I stood still a moment, my ears ringing from the shot, my mind working over what I'd done. I wondered why Nick hadn't fired. Just now he was emerging from the timber, headed toward the motionless bull. He carried his rifle at port arms as if expecting the bull to leap up and shoot back. I unloaded my rifle and placed the cartridges in my front pants pocket. I picked up my pack and walked onto the lake.

"Hey, we got some meat," Nick said, a big smile across his face. I asked why he hadn't shot. He said that he hadn't seen them. Hadn't seen two caribou on a half-mile wide lake? "Nope, didn't see 'em." He hadn't even seen the cow race across the lake after my shot.

Already the bull was bloating. I took off my parka and stuffed it into my pack. I got out my knife, fingered the edge and went to work. With Nick's help, I soon had the body open, heavy, scented, steam rising about us. Able to warm my hands on the steaming meat, I worked bare-handed. The bull was quickly gutted and the insides wiped with snow. The entrails and spilled blood froze almost at once. Before donning my mittens, I washed my hands in the snow and hurried them dry on the back of my pants.

Nick took the steel vacuum bottle from his pack and poured two cups of tepid sugared tea. I drank mine in two or three gulps and asked for more. I hadn't realized how thirsty I'd become.

"We should drag this one back to the car, then head south," Nick said. "It's after one already. In two hours it'll be dark. We can drive back to Glennallen and stay at that motel. Twelve bucks apiece, they said. We can try again tomorrow before heading home."

I quickly agreed, glad not to have to make the decisions. He was the one keen on getting a caribou, so it was best that he came up with the plan.

We looped a rope around the antlers, then, with gear stowed in packs and rifles over our backs, we both took grip on the rope and lunged down the lake. On packed snow or ice, the chore would have been easy, but here the carcass dug into the soft powder and it took real effort to keep it moving. Only after I put the rope over my shoulder could I match strength with Nick. It felt good to pull against the rope and struggle forward. I liked the common effort.

Now and again I'd look back at the carcass trailing blood splatters from the gut pile steaming faintly in the snow. I wondered how the lake, with its machine tracks, caribou trails, and red-purple viscera, must look from the air. Not a pretty picture, but killing—no matter the reason, no matter the victim—never is.

At first I felt smug. *You guys should try this. It's hunting. Not what you're doing. I worked for this meat, got it without a snowmachine.* I felt more certain when two machines roared by, faces flashing white in wonder, the look plain: *These guys are nuts.* I felt greater. Self-righteous.

Then I began to consider. Am I really better? Have I done anything different? Several caribou have died since we came here. Does it matter how? The snowmachiners hunted legally, broke no law. So what's wrong? They killed; I killed. They wanted meat; I wanted meat. This bull cared not *how* the bullet came to kill him, only that it did. It took one man two minutes, a pint of gasoline, and two bullets to kill one caribou. It took me four hours of cold, hard work, and one bullet to kill one caribou. Net result: two dead caribou.

The smugness faded. Perhaps there was no difference. We were all alike. No one here *really* needed the meat. How much would this two-day trip cost in gasoline, food, a place to stay? One hundred dollars? Two hundred? The meat would end up costing less than a dollar per pound, far cheaper than beef, yet that same money could buy a lot of rice and beans. I was struggling across the lake, through calf-deep snow, for a multitude of reasons, some obvious, others obscure. Hunting had always seemed a simple pursuit, but I was coming to realize its complexity, its ambiguity.

Several times we stopped to rest and catch our breath. For me, this was what it was all about. I'd grown up to believe hunting meant work. Work being the cost, the real license to kill. Alaskan hunters used planes, snowmachines, boats, airboats, and ATVs of all description not just for transport but as an integral part of hunting. This was an aberration to me. When challenged, such hunters defend the mechanization as being necessitated by the demands of the country. But if true, why did these snowmachiners hunt right next to the highway? Why did pilots fly around to spot game, then land nearby for an easy shot?

After a break at midlake we followed a machine trail and didn't stop again until we got onto the road, pulling right by the smirking snowmachiners, two more caribou on the ground by their tent.

Nick drove the car from the highway. We tied the caribou over the roof of the VW and headed south. Two hours later, in a blizzard, we pulled into Glennallen.

Next morning, before light, and after a good sleep on a poor mattress and a breakfast of toast, eggs, hash browns, pancakes, orange juice and coffee, plus a side of French toast for Nick, we drove north on the Richardson and turned east on the Tok cutoff.

In the first ten miles we saw only one car coming from Tok and we passed one semitrailer crawling up a steep, icy, hill. This day again was warm and cloudy with a few large flakes swirling down. Before full daylight we passed Gakona Roadhouse, a store and lodge, first built in 1905 as Doyle's Ranch. East of Gakona village we saw the first caribou trails crossing the road. Here the migration route shifted south toward the wintering grounds along the flanks of the Wrangell Mountains. We drove past a few parked cars. To judge by the accumulated snow, most had been parked for some time, perhaps by people who lived in cabins off the road. We saw no hunters.

On the summit of a low hill at Mile 105 we pulled off into a plowed turnout. Below us the Copper River snaked its way southwest through a vast snowy patchwork of spruce forest and lake-dotted bog. In the distance the massive timbered flanks of Mount Sanford climbed into the clouds. A light breeze soughed in the trees; a magpie called somewhere from the forest below.

"Look!" Nick all but yelled, pointing down at the river. A single file of caribou turned from the timber and out onto the river. They kept coming. The first few were bulls, with absurdly huge racks sweeping up from their small heads. I counted by twos. Ninety-seven caribou migrating toward the high plateaus around Mount Sanford. Perhaps half, maybe more, were bulls; the rest were cows. Oddly, none seemed to be calves. The first few animals moved deliberately, heads craning to search for danger. The others followed placidly, head to tail, content to plod away the miles. The leaders came to an open lead and after only a momentary hesitation, plunged in and swam easily to the far bank. The following caribou traversed the three-quarter-mile-wide riverbed and disappeared slowly into the timber. Just two miles from the road, they were safe from hunters.

A car pulled in behind us. The passengers took a long look at the caribou tied across the VW, then looked at the river, saw nothing and drove away.

This was the first big herd either of us had seen, and we stood staring down at the river. The sinuous trail mocked us. *Do you believe it? Were the caribou really there?* The empty, still land whispered *no*. The tracks screamed *yes. Caribou. Caribou on the river.*

We got in the car and drove on. Five miles from the Native village of Chistochina, at a place where the highway angled down to the river's edge, we parked in a pullout. I hid my rifle under a blanket on the backseat, content to be a pack animal.

We stepped off the road and fought through the snow berm and into the thick timber, Nick leading the way toward the river. Close to the road we found fresh beds, droppings, and the tracks of many caribou. Nick went ahead, rifle ready. Long after he'd gone from sight, I followed his progress by listening for the loud scrape of nylon and the crunch of snow.

Suddenly a shot, then another. I heard heavy movement, brush snapping, the sounds of stampeding animals. The caribou came running out of the timber right at me, the wide-eyed leaders shying away from me, splitting the group in two as they dashed by. I saw only two clearly; the others were mere brown and gray shadows streaking through the spruce. In a moment they were gone.

Nick called from close by. "I got one. Hey, Tom, I got one." I followed his trail, shaking my head at how easy it had been. A five-minute hunt, one hundred fifty yards from the road. An anticlimax. I wondered if he'd be pleased.

Nick grinned over a cow heaped against a twisted spruce. He laughed aloud as I struggled up. He shook my hand like an underdog politician running for office. Now we had meat, he said, and all so easy. *Too easy.*

In fifteen minutes we were hands and arms to the elbows inside the caribou. Two hours later we were back at the car wondering where to put the new load. Half an hour later, after a little judicious sawing, we were headed back toward Anchorage with one caribou frozen on the roof and another, minus lower legs, cooling in the backseat.

II

Caribou hunting was like that in 1966. Several huge herds roamed across major highways and at certain times of the year were vulnerable to hunters. This was a time of transition. The snowmachine, the "iron dog," was new to the country. At first, wildlife managers praised the machines, hoping the mobility would spread out the harvest and bring hunters to the more inaccessible herds in need of culling.

Not every hunt along the road system was a sure thing, but usually caribou were numerous and easily accessible to the highway. In fact, road hunting—driving back and forth along a section of highway until a moose or caribou stepped out—was one of the most popular ways to "hunt."

An estimated six hundred thousand caribou, in six major herds plus eight smaller ones, roamed the Alaska tundra. Two herds, the Nelchina and the Steese-Fortymile, bore the brunt of the urban population's demand for sport and meat. At various times, when the herds crossed the Steese and Taylor highways, the Glenn, Richardson, and Denali highways, or Lake Louise Road, the long guns boomed, the snowmachines growled, and the caribou died in large numbers.

Before the advent of the snowmachine and before Alaska's human population began to expand, there was little fear of overharvest. Almost overnight the snowmachine changed the equation, and before anyone could sound the alarm, some herds, notably the Nelchina, were in trouble.

In late August each of the first five or six years I lived in Alaska, when darkness returned with the glitter of frost and blazing tundra, I hunted caribou for meat. Struggling financially, trying to make a life not tied to the nine-to-five, and later with the beginnings of a family, I hunted near the road. The Nelchina. Lake Louise. The Fortymile. The Denali. God's Country, we called the high tundra near the McLaren and Susitna rivers. One year I hunted the Nabesna, driving to the end of the road, searching the piedmont and north face of the Wrangells for caribou and moose. One winter I hunted Paxson Lake, from old Doc Huffman's, killing a nice young bull two miles south of his cabin. He ranted about the devastation being wrought by snowmachines and sniped at the biologists for not stopping it.

Another year I hunted the Taylor Highway and left early, disgusted by the swarm of hunters down from Fairbanks and the military bases. Many had no regard for the animals. They shot into herds, they left kills in the brush and gutpiles in the roadway, they flouted the law. It was the worst I'd ever witnessed, worse even than the firing line in the old days. The turnouts above the beautiful sweep of high country looked like camper parks. Dead caribou everywhere.

By the midseventies illegal and unethical hunting on the Taylor Highway became so blatant that the state launched Operation Caribou, a high-visibility program designed to curtail the abuse.

The season and bag limits of the preceding years had been liberal. South of the Yukon River, the season ran from August until March with a three-caribou, either sex, bag limit. North of the Yukon, the season was open year-round with no limit on the number that could be killed.

In 1966 the State of Alaska was only six years old, with a population of two hundred and fifty thousand. Oil had yet to be discovered on the North Slope, and the economy was feeble. Conventional wisdom then had it that Dall sheep and brown–grizzly bears faced an uncertain future because of heavy demand by trophy hunters, but moose and caribou would always provide an abundance of meat for Alaskan larders. A moose, because it provided a large quantity of good meat, was prized, but the ubiquitous caribou supplied more families.

As easy as it was to obtain a caribou, it nonetheless bothered me to hear someone say: "This year I killed only a caribou." *Only* a caribou? In function and form, this creature is among the most exquisite of all wild animals.

The name *caribou* comes from the Canadian Indian name *Xalibu*, the "pawer," a reference to the way the animal uncovers lichens hidden beneath the snow. The caribou's most important adaptation to the northern environment may be its ability to subsist on lichens, primitive plants that grow well on poor tundra soils. Caribou locate their food by smell, thrusting their noses into the snow as they walk along. Even the scientific name, *Rangifer tarandus*, "the wanderer," speaks of far, arctic lands.

In its sleek summer pelage, a caribou dancing over the tundra displays supple grace and strength refined over the centuries by the harsh boreal environment, long migrations, and numerous predators.

In autumn, the dark summer coat is replaced by rich brown and white. A big bull is particularly beautiful. In contrast to the white belly, the lower legs are almost fudge brown, with the black, crescent hooves fringed in long brown and white hair. Where the legs join the body, an inch-wide line of white hair laterally bisects the coat from neck to flank. The rump and underside of the short tail, which raises to warn of danger, are white, surrounded by brown. In sharp contrast to the white rut-swollen neck and throat ruff, the saddleback behind the withers can be almost auburn. The head, except for the white muzzle, inside ears, and circles about the eyes, is a dark brown. In summer and early spring, ragged patches of moulting hair hang from the coat, but in autumn the entire pelt looks rich and curried.

In winter the pelage changes to a tight layer of long, hollow guard hairs over a coat of fine, curly wool that allows undiminished function even in the most severe wind, cold, and snow.

If this elegant pelage were not remarkable enough, caribou bulls sport impressive antlers. From small, gnarled bases in front of the ears, slender main beams swoop backward then forward in a graceful crescent. The beams can spread over sixty inches at the widest point. The top end of each beam flattens into a palm eight or nine inches wide with a half-dozen or more rapier-like tines. These fighting tines can be over a foot long. Midway on the main beams and pointing backward are single tines seven or eight inches long. A few inches up from the bases curve multitined eyeguards called bez points, or bay antlers. And, on the biggest bulls, at the base of each antler, growing forward like spades on edge, extending sometimes even beyond the end of the muzzle, are enormous palms, called shovels.

These huge racks look disproportionately large for the caribou's small head and slender body. Posing on a ridge, its antlers free of velvet, tine tips gleaming like ivory, throat ruff rustling in the wind, a big bull truly is stunning.

Given this extraordinary elegance, the low regard some hunters have for caribou astounds me. Only after the accessible herds declined markedly did a caribou kill become notable. Caribou had always been easy to get and prized more for meat than for looks. Perhaps if the bag limit had been one animal instead of three or more, caribou would not have been taken for granted and the privilege of hunting them abused.

In Alaska any time a multiple bag limit was established for big game some people responded with contempt. Instead of respect for an individual animal, the focus became killing the bag limit even if the meat was unneeded.

Caribou were looked down upon not only because of their abundance but because they seemed dull-witted. Granted, a caribou does not possess the wariness of the grizzly, the intelligence of a wolf, or the stealth of an elk. Often a caribou will allow a hunter to walk or drive up within rifle range. Once spooked, or even after being shot at, a caribou might make a wide-sweeping circle and come running right back. Like pronghorns of the western plains, caribou can be flagged in. Their curiosity can be a fatal weakness. Once I tied a handkerchief on a long stick and waved it from behind a bush and lured two caribou within camera range.

Unlike white-tailed deer, caribou do not have a keenly developed fear of man. A caribou will stand and watch danger approach and rely on its speed for protection. Caribou understand pursuit and find comfort in exposed places where they can watch for the enemy. They react as herd animals react: if one flees, they all flee. When alarmed, a caribou leaps, rearing on its hind feet, a small gland near the rear hooves giving off a warning scent. Other caribou coming upon the point of the excitation leap will detect the scent and react in kind.

In the summer caribou can appear deranged. One minute a caribou will stand motionless, the next, without any apparent provocation, it may dash off across the tundra as if all hell's wolves were in pursuit. Then, just as abruptly, it may stop, stand still a moment, then rush off in a mad dash in the opposite direction. This can go on for hours. In a way, the animal *is* crazy—driven mad by any number of insect pests. Mosquitoes attack relentlessly. Warble flies burrow under the skin to lay their eggs. Huge balls of fly larvae may writhe within a caribou's sinuses.

Crazy? Exactly.

III

In the sixties I hunted often in God's Country. The Denali Highway, built in the 1950s as an access route to Mount McKinley National Park, later renamed Denali National Park, bisected the Nelchina Basin, then some of the best wildlife habitat in Alaska. Stretching from Cantwell to Paxson Roadhouse on the Richardson Highway, the rugged gravel road attracted hunters and fishermen from everywhere. I loved the country around Tangle Lakes and the McLaren River valley. Caribou were common but so were moose and ptarmigan. Once from the road by Tangle Lakes I even spotted a grizzly feeding on blueberries. Grayling fishing in the area was excellent.

One autumn I hunted the Denali with Larry and Gary Baker. We stayed at Butcher's Camp, a collection of small cabins overlooking Upper Tangle Lake. We arrived late at night to a hard frost and stars sparkling in an ebony sky. Next morning, before dawn, the Bakers hiked off across the tundra to the southeast, while I went west. The day dawned clear but the sun had little warmth; the ice on the ponds finally melted just before ten.

The tundra rolled into the foothills and I wandered with no particular route or plan in mind. Each autumn day, a movement toward snow, was to be savored and enjoyed. I hiked slowly, enjoying the autumn smells, the distant sounds of geese and cranes passing overhead, and the occasional flush of ptarmigan broods grown to maturity. I gazed at distant, snow-lined peaks, or at far tundra horizons.

I can't say that I hunted much. I spent most of my time eating blueberries and relaxing in these last moments of sunshine still strong enough to warm my back and shoulders. I'd learned that the finest autumnal gift is a bright sun on a windless afternoon. The fading leaves whispered of winter, a winter seven months long.

Twice during the day I heard gunfire boom across the hills. I looked with my binoculars but saw nothing. Even the highway and camp was beyond the rolling hills.

Just after dark I was the first to the cabin. Anticipating my friends' imminent arrival, I made dinner. I waited as long as I could, then ate without them. The leftovers grew cold. Two hours after dark they came in. Larry's jeans were bloodied and he did not have his pack.

"I'm hungry," Larry said. "Let's eat." I put the food and the teapot on to heat.

"Larry got a caribou on that ridge east of the lake, a small bull," Gary said. "The meat's hung in the screened shed."

"Heard the shooting. I wondered if that was you guys."

"Did you hear shots about two hours ago, just at dark?" Gary asked. "Larry got a moose near a little pond. A big bull, too, and only a quarter-mile off the road."

This was good news: meat for the families. Larry was scraping by, trying to succeed as a self-employed taxidermist. To make ends meet, he worked summers for various resource agencies. Gary was a load master on Hercules aircraft for Alaska Airlines.

Larry said that he shot the caribou in early afternoon on a ridge just east of Upper Tangle Lake. While packing the meat to the road, the brothers spotted the bull moose feeding at the edge of the pond. They had gutted the moose in the gathering darkness and had walked home on the road. We had to go back after dinner to butcher and pack in the meat. Left until morning, the moose could be claimed by a grizzly.

After dinner we loaded the car with packs and butchering tools and drove off into the black night. One and a half miles east of the Tangle Lakes bridge, Larry stopped his sedan at the side of the road where he'd stacked rocks to mark the route to the dead moose. We shouldered packs and stumbled off into the dark brush. Hardly able to see a thing, we wandered around for what seemed an hour before finding the moose. Larry said he found it by smell. I didn't doubt that.

Hampered as we were by darkness, the butchering took a long time. I did little more than hold up a leg or pull on the hide. Sometime after midnight we began packing small loads of meat to the car. After a couple of light loads, we learned a good route through the brush. On my first trip with a heavy load, a hindquarter, I tripped and fell backward into a shallow, brushy depression. Like an upended tortoise, I struggled futilely to rise. My mutterings flared into the fire of swearing out loud. Over at the moose I heard Larry talking.

"Do you hear something, Gary? No? It's probably just the wind."

I shut up. I lay on my back catching my breath. Stars glittered in the ebony night. To the southwest Orion swung his sword high, hunting Leo, or the Great Bear, or me. The Pleiades glinted like a multifaceted jewel. I located Cassiopeia, daughter of Andromeda, and Polaris, the North Star.

I shrugged out of the pack and got up. I pulled the load from the depression, sat down, wiggled into the harness and struggled to my feet. In a short while I was to the road.

Around three in the morning the northern lights came out, illuminating the ground. No longer did we stumble through the brush. At one point we watched three enormous curtains of light stretching from horizon to horizon. The tundra foothills were as bright as under a full moon.

"Who could deny God after they've seen this?" said Larry, a devout Lutheran.

I thought then of the sourdough who described the aurora as the combined spirits of animals and man dancing in the cold. I thanked the moose and the caribou for the meat.

With the light, we were able to get to bed by four o'clock.

Late the next afternoon I walked into the coulees west of Tangle Lakes. Twice I saw caribou at a distance. I saw a cow moose feeding in a pond. From a ridgetop I watched a fox hunting the willows below. He seemed to be stalking ptarmigan. In front of a sere clump of grass, he came to a point, not unlike that of a sporting dog. I expected a bird to flush but instead the fox took one halting step, then jumped straight up and landed hard on his front feet, his head jabbing into the grass. In a second he trotted away, a vole clamped in his jaws.

A congratulatory cheer died in my throat. I felt something watching me and turned to see a caribou forty yards away. She had come over the ridge and surprised me kneeling in the brush. I raised my rifle and sighted on her neck. After a moment I lowered the gun and watched her crow-hop away. This wasn't the time.

IV

I've hunted and photographed caribou all over Alaska. I've brought home winter meat from Becharof Lake, Ptarmigan Valley, Mystic Creek, Goldking, and the John River. I last hunted near a road in 1970. I decided then to hunt remote areas, to work harder for my meat and antlers, to see new country. Too, I wanted not to be a part of what was happening in those more accessible regions.

Mostly I hunted on foot, slogging along in hipboots or snowshoes. Only once, in 1970, did I hunt from the road using a snowmachine. I was hunting the Denali with John Liska, then a taxidermist, later a state representative. I got a small bull and dragged it in behind the machine. We'd driven back away from the road and parked the machine before hunting but even at twenty below, the ease of the whole venture made it something less than satisfying.

Some of the best hunts were conducted with the aid of horses. Before coming to Alaska I'd worked as a wrangler and guide in California's eastern Sierra, taking dudes into the John Muir Wilderness Area. Though the boggy muskeg could not compare with the Forest Service's manicured trail system, a horse could take a person where no plane, all-terrain vehicle, or four-wheel-drive could go. A horse, or even a string of horses, did not seem to frighten moose or caribou. In fact, I've heard stories of bull moose expressing an amorous interest in mares during the rut, with predictably disastrous results.

Horse hunting was not easy. In fact, it meant two extra hours of work per day in care and feeding of stock. No matter how tired I was, the horses came first.

I seldom actually hunted from horseback, preferring to leave the animals in camp until after the kill, then using them to pack in the meat. In 1971, near Mystic Creek, I helped John Thuma kill a nice bull caribou. I loaded the meat-filled panniers on Hank, a bay packhorse. He didn't like the smell of wild meat, so I moved very slowly, calming him as I worked. With great caution I laid the caribou rack on top of the sawbucks. All went well until I reached back for the pack rope. Hank had moved a little, and stretch as I might, I couldn't reach the rope. Since Hank was standing peacefully, I let go of the rack and bent down for the rope. In that split second the rack slowly tipped backward. I leaped away just as the tines jabbed Hank in the rump. He exploded, rearing and kicking at the demon jabbing him from the rear. The antlers slumped down over his rump sending him into orbit. Each time he kicked and bucked, the tines poked him all the more. I could do nothing but stand and watch until the antlers finally bucked free. In an arc they went up, then down, to be met with a perfectly timed kick of both hind feet. The antlers went hurtling into the brush.

Thuma stood there cackling like a fool. I didn't think it was so funny. Now Hank was really shy, and I was the one who had to reload the panniers and antlers. Two hours later, with the aid of a blindfold and an extra-long rope, I had the load in place.

After that Hank shied whenever he saw a caribou.

V

In the late sixties unsettling rumors filtered out from Interior Alaska: the big herds were no more.

The Steese-Fortymile herd, said to have numbered half a million animals in the hazy past, began a steady decline in the 1930s. Still, as late as 1960 swarms of caribou passed close to Fairbanks on their migration eastward to the wintering grounds near Dawson City. But in the late 1960s the herd dropped to twenty thousand, and in the 1970s it hit a low of five thousand.

The demise of the Steese-Fortymile herd was gradual. The crash of the Nelchina herd, however, was sudden and dramatic. In 1964 this herd, perhaps one of the most important because of its accessibility to both Anchorage and Fairbanks, numbered around ninety thousand animals. Less than ten years later pessimists estimated that only eight thousand caribou ranged the Nelchina piedmont.

Fingers were pointed: Damn wolves. Snowmachines. Overhunting. The damn fish and game people.

But guilt could not be so easily established as that. Diminished range caused by wildfires and overgrazing by the caribou themselves, severe winter weather, poor calf survival rates, predation, overhunting, radical herd movements and splintering, game management blunders, and natural population fluctuations—all combined to create the disaster.

For years biologists had been warning that the Nelchina herd faced trouble. As early as 1954, when the herd was reaching one-third its 1960s peak, the U.S. Fish and Wildlife Service predicted that because unchecked growth was putting pressure on the winter range, caribou might move or die. Indeed, before the decline was fully documented a biologist reported monitoring the unusual migration into Canada of a large segment of the herd, which apparently never returned to its former range. Some biologists now doubt that emigrations to other ranges played a significant part in the decline.

In a short time in the sixties, biologists went from decrying the dangers of overpopulation to hushed talk of disaster. Because the range had deteriorated while the caribou population expanded, biologists were looking for ways to increase the harvest. At a 1967 state Game Division meeting, biologists listened to a report on how the snowmachine could be an important tool—but no one could foresee its impact. In 1972, during a winter of deep snow when many calves perished, the Nelchina herd also sustained a record harvest of 9,128. In October 1973, biologists counted the herd and estimated a total population of 8,136. That year hunters killed only 555 caribou.

Without doubt overhunting—coupled with poor calf survival—played an important part in the decline. In winter, just when caribou were most vulnerable, snowmachines made hunting easy and efficient. The liberal seasons and bag limits, which had been appropriate until the coming of the snowmachine and the human population boom sparked by the 1968 North Slope oil discovery, were changed too late. (Scientists argue still whether the increased calf mortality levels were due to winter weather–induced starvation or winter-aided predation.)

Another game management blunder occurred earlier, before statehood, when the U.S. Fish and Wildlife Service decimated the predators. Field biologists had been warning of deteriorating range caused by over-abundant caribou. Yet administrators, for political rather than biological reasons, continued poisoning wolves to control predation. Some people now wonder what might have happened had the wolf-caribou interplay not been so radically upset. Clearly, confrontation between field biologists and administrators continues. Management decisions are often made because of political considerations contrary to the findings of field managers and researchers.

At statehood in 1959 the Alaska Department of Fish and Game took over wildlife management from the U.S. Fish and Wildlife Service. Though many of the same biologists worked for both agencies, policies changed. The federal service had carried out a massive poisoning and control effort in the Nelchina Basin, radically reducing wolves in the area. The fledgling state agency stopped the program.

Later, when the wolf population had recovered but caribou were still declining, predation may have accelerated the decline, but even under the scrutiny of twenty-twenty hindsight, no one can say for certain.

The 1975 crash of the western arctic caribou herd is an interesting case. Unlike the Nelchina herd, these caribou roamed remote wildlands. In spring, postcalving aggregations in the tens of thousands formed in the northern drainages of the Delong Mountains. The herds summered on the North Slope's coastal plain and Brooks Range piedmont, and wintered on the Selawik and Buckland river drainages, the coastal plain, the central Brooks Range, and as far west as the eastern Seward Peninsula.

When the herd collapsed from two hundred fifty thousand to sixty thousand animals, fingers were pointed at the same old suspects, most notably wolves and game managers. This time, however, the situation was more complex, and more volatile. The western arctic caribou herd was hunted almost exclusively by Alaska Natives.

Since earliest times caribou have sustained arctic peoples, supplying not only meat for humans and dogs, but also fat for lights and cooking; hides for tents, sleeping robes, clothing, footgear, and boats; bone for needles,

scrapers, and fish hooks; sinew for sewing. Even today, caribou are important to Natives for practical, cultural, and aesthetic reasons. Because recreational hunting by outsiders was minimal, the decline of the western arctic
herd was at first blamed on overharvest by rural subsistence hunters.

Alaska's newly expanded media base covered every twinge of the state's
growing pains, especially wildlife issues: sport hunting versus subsistence
hunting, rural rights versus urban rights. The issue of hunting rights and
responsibilities, thanks in part to the distortion inherent in media coverage,
became an almost racial issue pitting Natives against whites.

Native leaders were unwilling to admit that questionable but common-
place hunting practices contributed to the decline. Many Native hunters
favor .22 caliber firearms. I have heard villagers call a .22 a good all-around
gun because it can be used to shoot hares, ptarmigan, ducks, marine
mammals, and big game. Unfortunately, such a small bullet will not consis-
tently kill large animals cleanly. Many times, without showing signs of
having been shot, a caribou runs off, only to die a lingering death.

Caching caribou in the field, another common Native practice, led to
charges of widespread, wanton waste. Often, dead caribou were left behind
in the field. It could not be denied that some hunters never intended to go
back for the meat at all, but even hunters with the best intentions to return
lost a portion to wolves, wolverines, foxes, ravens, and spoilage.

Some Natives did not know when to stop shooting. A Fish and
Wildlife officer once told me of a hunt he'd been invited to join when he
lived in a coastal Native village. The hunters, on snowmachines, encountered a large number of caribou a few miles from town. The man who had
invited the officer on the trip began shooting into the herd, and quite
legally, killed twenty-one caribou. The ungutted animals were collected,
and each hunter dragged one caribou behind his machine back to town.
Although the officer pleaded and cajoled, the hunter eventually salvaged
the meat of only five animals. (No local magistrate or jury would ever
convict a villager on game violations. No charges were filed.)

Many Native people have strong traditional prohibitions against waste.
Custom calls for paying proper respect to an animal and using all its parts to
avoid offending its spirit. A pragmatism works here as well: a majority of
older Natives all too painfully remember lean times and empty stomachs.
Unfortunately, however, a caribou left to rot feeds no one.

The year before the crash of the western arctic caribou herd made
headlines, I flew over an area in the Brooks Range just west of a Native

village. I saw more than a hundred caribou dead in the snow. I doubted many of them would be salvaged. Some villages lived by the traditional ethic and wasted nothing, but this village was not among them. Here was a vivid example of the sliding away of the old values, of wildlife caught in the crosscurrent of change.

Caribou could be killed at any time of the year without regard to sex or age; the meat and hides could be sold, bartered, or used as dog food. Critics likened these practices to those that caused the extirpation of bison from the western plains. In 1973 a pilot who lived year-round in the Brooks Range submitted a proposal to the Alaska Board of Game to modify the hunting practices north of the Yukon River: to limit the kill to seven animals per person, to close the season during calving, and to place some restrictions on the sale of caribou meat.

Immediately the proposal came under fire from Natives, by then growing powerful from the influx of oil wealth and the settlement of their aboriginal land claims. Inherent in the proposal was the implication that subsistence users had damaged the resource. No Native leader was willing to make such an admission. Attorneys schooled in the liberal traditions of civil rights activism but new to Alaska eloquently represented Native interests. Many of these lawyers saw the confrontation over subsistence hunting rights as a logical extension of the civil rights movement. As well-intentioned as many were, most had no knowledge of the dynamics of wildlife management. Though many counterproposals had potentially disastrous implications for wildlife, I never once heard an attorney address the animals' welfare. The real civil rights of Natives, as of all Alaskans, would have been best served by the protection and enhancement of the wildlife.

Caribou were vital to Native villagers, and they did not want any restrictions on hunting. "With these changes," they said, "our children will go hungry." That was a point hard to contest. No one wanted people to suffer or children to starve. Villagers who watched big herds pass by saw no need for change—but they saw only a small part of the picture.

The Alaska Department of Fish and Game was slow to respond. By autumn 1975, when the evidence of the crash could no longer be disputed, emergency regulations were enacted to prevent further decline. For 1976, among other restrictions, hunting was by permit only; the bag limit was reduced to one bull per person; sale and barter were curtailed. And a wolf-control program was implemented.

The state's game managers were again in the vortex of controversy, vilified by all sides for failing to prevent the disaster. But it was not through malfeasance or incompetence that they had failed to take action: they were hampered by the size and inaccessibility of the area, the lack of field staff, the heat of political pressure, and the unpredictable effects of the many factors at work. The result, however, was the same as for the Nelchina caribou. In a very short time, men using snowmachines and following wasteful hunting practices had decimated parts of the herd.

Partially because of the collapse of the western arctic caribou and the continuation of unpopular wolf-control efforts, the Alaska Department of Fish and Game has not enjoyed a good reputation or been trusted by many residents, even though it employs some of the finest professional biologists in the world. Even as Alaskan wildlife was subjected to diminishing habitat, land use conflicts, and increased hunting pressure, however, the Game Division budget was being cut by the state legislature. In the future, if any important segment of the wildlife resource declines, the department will find itself in a catch-22: it will be blamed for inaction by those who, by withholding the necessary funds, made action impossible.

Subsistence hunting is apple pie and motherhood for Alaskan politicians. But it is a horrendously complex issue, and no one can agree on the terms. Many who must hunt for food also enjoy the sport. And those who hunt for recreation also value the meat. There are good and bad elements in both groups. I have seen sport hunters waste meat; I have seen subsistence hunters waste meat. I have also seen the races polarized. It is a sad thing.

Both the state and the federal government have wrestled with the subsistence hunting issue. Special-interest groups lobby to push their own proposals, often without regard for others or for the wildlife. Many times the participants find themselves in court. The legal tangles are not easily undone, with frightening ramifications for wildlife and people alike.

In the late 1980s the Nelchina caribou herd grew to over thirty thousand and the once vast Steese-Fortymile herd approached twenty thousand — gradual and closely monitored recovery. By 1985 draconian management measures, plus education and information programs, had aided the recovery of the western arctic herd. By the end of the decade it numbered over three hundred seventy-five thousand and was still expanding.

Unfortunately, it seems we are unable to look at the past, even the recent past, and recognize our errors. Wildlife resources are not limitless, and not capable of withstanding sustained abuse. When the trans-Alaska pipeline was built, big-game hunting north of the Yukon River was prohibited within five miles of it, and mechanized access across it for the purposes of hunting was made illegal. Although the law was later changed to allow bowhunting, the original intent—to protect local wildlife—remained the same.

Before long the law was abused. In the 1980s it was all but ignored. North of Atigun Pass, illegal riflemen on snowmachines killed caribou well within the closed area and, at times, right next to the pipeline. The lawbreaking appeared widespread and the toll on wildlife, excessive.

Sidney Huntington, an Athabascan and long-time member of the committee of appointees who set Alaska's game laws, has wrestled with the issues for many years. Although he has described himself as "a dumb Indian with a third-grade education," he is anything but. His support of wolf-control efforts has been controversial, but he has often been the only one heard to say: "First it must be good for the wildlife. Then it will be good for whites and Natives alike."

VI

Some Natives still live in the old way. They accord caribou almost religious reverence: *tuktu*, the provider. Meat. Hide. Utensils. Sinew. Caribou are part of the old way, the good way, the understandable way. Caribou hunting is a simple, joyful reason to live, if not a mystical experience.

Iñuuniaġniq allaŋŋuqtuq

The way of life is changing.

Young John lived in a village in the Brooks Range, in a difficult valley. A strong, good-humored man, he had suffered much. One year his small daughter contracted spinal meningitis and, for lack of proper treatment, went blind. She was sent to a children's home in Anchorage. Another year, his wife left him for a white man, left him with a daughter in a far place and a small son at home. Soon his wife died, overdosed on the white man's drugs.

The next year, one day in spring, Young John did what was for him an uncommon thing. He drank too much. That night he went into the steam house. He asked someone leaving to add fuel to the fire. The last thing he remembers is throwing water on the rocks to make steam. The next day, burned in the conflagration, he was medivac'd to Anchorage. He lost a leg and spent eight months enduring pain, healing tissues, and learning to use an artificial limb.

He would call home to speak with his son. There was only one phone in the village. "Dad, when are you coming home?" his son would ask. He could not say.

He said the nightmares were the worst: months of dreams about burning up.

He wanted to go home. See his son. Take him caribou hunting.

When the leaves turned gold and started to fall, he brightened. It was time to leave and prepare for the hunt. Already the caribou would be in the pass. But he stayed in Anchorage. The land froze and winter came. He looked disheartened.

By the time he went home, competent on his artificial leg, the caribou had passed through and were gone. He'd missed the first caribou hunt of his adult life. The winter would be long and hungry.

VII

In my youth I dreamed of herds of caribou, vast waves rolling over the tundra. Like scenes from the American plains of the 1800s. Thousands of animals: cows, calves, bulls. Forests of antlers. Caribou trotting click-footed over the sedge, lichen, tussock lowlands. Wolves trailing the herds, waiting for young calves and stragglers.

North of the Arctic Circle, on the very edge of the arctic ice, the dream of a youth became reality. Each spring on the tundra prairies north of the Brooks Range, between the Canning and Kongakut rivers, the Porcupine caribou herd assembles in huge calving aggregations, a hundred and fifty thousand animals in all. One spring I flew from Barter Island into the Arctic National Wildlife Refuge to observe and shoot photographs.

Flying to my destination, I could look back at the arctic ice pack stretching unbroken to the pole, then ahead to the south where the Brooks Range massif reared above the coastal plain—a plain so flat that in winter, when it is covered with snow, you would be hard pressed to tell where land ended and the sea ice began.

The tundra, by now mostly clear of snow and ice, was a drab, dried-grass brown. Ponds, marshes, rivulets, and creeks glinted silver in the sun. Overflow ice still blocked the deltas of the major waterways, but the brown runoff was rapidly cutting channels through it.

We flew over bands of caribou, groups of several dozen animals each. The adult caribou, bleached by the bright spring sun that already hung in the sky twenty-four hours a day, were easy to see. Once in a while I saw a reddish calf following at its mother's heels. I felt the old thrill. *The calving grounds of the Porcupine herd.* Home of the barren-ground grizzly, the tundra wolf, the snowy owl, the peregrine falcon, the musk-ox.

Long after the bush plane had left, I stood on the gravel bar airstrip, staring into the distance. A low fog off the ice pack advanced, the brown sunlight burning like a slow fire enveloped in its own smoke. The herds were to the east.

I walked to the river. The closer I got, the louder the roar. From bank to bank charging, roiling snowmelt was rushing north to the Arctic Ocean. Standing waves swelled at the underlying rock, and now and then I heard a loud *pop*, as if two giant bowling balls were clacking together: the river was tearing boulders loose and sending them smashing downstream. *Boulders,* not rocks. I had planned to wade the river to the west side and follow the herds to perhaps Camden Bay, but I would have to wait.

A few hours later, as the cold fog rolled over the land and blotted out the sun, I crawled into the two-man tent I'd pitched in the willows and went to sleep. Sometime that night my watch quit. In the days to come I lost orientation to a time-regulated schedule. The sun never set but merely circled the sky.

After two days of exploring the country near the airstrip, I moved camp downriver ten miles. I set up my tent below a bluff where Inuit had camped. Kicking through the rubble left behind, I found two large cans with the labels intact: WILD MAINE BLUEBERRIES.

Late that day the wind picked up and wet snow began falling. I climbed into the tent to wait out the storm. Twice during the next hours I awoke to knock snow from the tent. Much later—I can't say whether it was the same day, that night, or the next day—I was awakened by strange sounds coming from all around the tent. I'd never heard anything like it before.

Cautiously I unzipped the tent door and poked my head out. Snow was still falling, and the ground was covered with a thick, wet blanket. All around me were caribou. Cows with calves, cows alone, hundreds of them. At once I realized the tent was camouflaged by the fallen snow. Some animals pawed the snow just feet from me.

Anxious cows trotted back and forth, muttering for their errant calves. Tiny calves trotted in circles bleating for their mothers. When mother and calf were reunited, the calf would rush forth with a loud cry and almost at once begin to nurse.

Caribou in the fall are vocal. The bulls' hoarse coughing sounds are variously described as grunting, snorting, roaring, or panting. Indeed, the word *rut* comes from a Latin word meaning "to roar." The sound made by these cows and calves was a nonstop cross between the bleating of a lamb and the lowing of a dairy cow. It seemed that the few lone cows were the only ones not in constant agitation.

The reddish-brown calves were everywhere. Apparently most of the calving had already taken place. Except for a few barren cows, many cows still had one or both antlers. Unlike bulls, which shed their headgear in October and November, pregnant cows keep their antlers until calving time. Right after birth their antlers drop off. Barren cows lose their antlers during the long winter, beginning about the same time the bulls lose theirs.

A few young bulls wandered through the herd, easy to spot with their velvet stubs. The older, mature bulls were miles to the east, well behind the cow and calf aggregations.

The calves, though appearing thin and fragile, were extremely active. At times the little ones would play and chase each other at high speed, darting in and out through the herd. This play accounted for the separation between the cows and their calves. The smallest calves, perhaps the newborns, raced in circles about their mothers. Around and around they'd go with startling speed. It was nature's way of strengthening young bodies for challenges from predators and the rigors of the migration. Although only days apart in age, already some calves were noticeably larger than others. Nourished by the richest milk of any land animal, milk that contains twenty percent fat, the young ones grow rapidly.

The herd passed slowly by my tent and I drifted off to sleep to the music of the wind and talking caribou.

I awoke to silence. I looked out: the snow had stopped, the wind had died, and the sun burned through the char-belly-colored fog. The caribou were gone.

After breakfasting on granola and black tea, I gladly left the tent to climb the bluff to the east. Caribou tracks and droppings littered the ground. Through the binoculars I saw to the west a huge herd spread across the snowy plain. I tried counting but gave up. Thousands of animals had crossed the flooding river and I wondered how many of the tiny calves had been washed away.

A few days later I hid in the willows and watched another group of cows with young calves venture across the flood. Though buoyed by their hollow-haired coats and powered by broad hooves, the adults still had difficulty crossing. Most of the calves were swept downstream. All but one of the cows kept on going and never looked back, leaving the loudly bleating calves to make their own way across the torrent. One by one the tiny calves came ashore far downstream then raced off after the moving adults. The one cow that had stayed behind to call to her offspring ran to smell each calf as it struggled dripping from the water. Ironically, her calf drowned beneath a driftwood sweeper.

Behind me to the east I could see more caribou moving west. By accident I'd camped in the direct path of the migration of a main calving aggregation; a biologist for the Fish and Wildlife Service later estimated that twenty-five thousand caribou passed in the area of my camp. The feeble sun melted the snow and the small tent looked out of place on the lichen-covered tundra. It wasn't long before the herd was streaming over the bluff and passing by my tent. Though the nylon whipped and snapped in the stiffening wind, the caribou paid it little attention. I hid in the willows near the river and took pictures as the caribou forded the torrent.

Bluff Camp, as I called it, became a favorite. I was content to stay near camp to watch and photograph the waves of caribou. Each day I looked for a sign that the runoff was abating so that I could cross the river and follow the herds. But, despite a lack of precipitation, the water stayed high. Here I encountered two wildlife researchers who gave me the time and date. In clear weather I could chart the passage of a day by the circling sun, but often the weather was poor. This made telling time impossible, and knowing the day, a guess. The biologists would reorient me on another occasion, but when the plane finally came to get me, I thought it was morning; in reality it was late afternoon.

It took four days for the herds to pass by. On the fifth day I climbed the bluff behind camp and looked in all directions and saw nothing, not a single animal. Where once was an abundance of life, now was absence. I wanted desperately to cross the river, but though I went far upstream and downstream I could not find a place to cross.

Late in the evening, two days later, from atop the bluff I spotted on the west side of the river a long thin line moving upriver. At first I thought my eyes were playing tricks on me. It looked exactly like a giant caterpillar inching over the tundra. Though I knew it wasn't possible, I then thought I was looking at a long procession of bears. At that moment I realized that these creatures were musk-ox.

Head to tail the long line moved slowly upriver and past my camp. Their rich brown and white coats were so long that I could neither see legs and feet, nor tell head from rump except by the direction the animals moved. In fact, the effect was otherworldly. I recalled my first impression. At a distance, individually and as a group, the musk-ox looked exactly like giant caterpillars. I could see humps at both ends, and at any moment I expected the caterpillar to reverse step and head back the way it had come. Never had I seen anything like it. With the possible exception of bison, the musk-ox resembled no other animal that I'd ever seen. Here was the Inuit's *oomingmak*, "the bearded one."

I went to bed that day with a sense of discouragement. I seemed trapped on the wrong side of the river. If the waters did not fall enough to wade, I would move downriver until I came to a crossing point, even if it meant hiking the thirty-odd miles to the delta.

The twenty-four hours of daylight and the absence of a regulating timepiece were disorienting. I'd get into my sleeping bag to warm up only to fall asleep. Sometime later I'd awake with a start and not know if I'd been asleep for minutes, hours, or a day. Other times I'd hike the tundra and be active for what seemed like days. While I waited to cross the river, the weather turned cold and stormy, forcing me to stay long hours in the tent. I learned about hibernation.

Finally after a long sleep I awoke to silence. No wind battered the tent, and the river was quiet. Excited, I pulled on my clothes and went to the river. The flood had subsided. I could cross.

The muddy water in midstream curled at the top of my hipboots. I moved carefully, feeling my way between the rocks. The current pushed at me, and without the eighty-pound pack I would have been swept off my feet. Past midstream the bottom began to rise and I easily gained the opposite shore. I was exhilarated. I could follow the caribou to the coast, find the musk-ox.

Once on the west bank I turned south and headed upstream. Musk-ox live only in remote portions of Alaska, and I wanted to see them up close before heading for the coast. These animals were part of a transplanted herd, the last of the original Alaskan musk-ox having fallen by 1850 to whalers, explorers, and Inuit with trade rifles. In 1935 and 1936 thirty-one Greenland musk-ox were released on Nunivak Island and they thrived. In the mid-1960s transplants were made to various island and mainland locations. In 1969 fifty-two musk-ox were flown to Barter Island and released. The animals I sought were their progeny.

Several hours later, I located the musk-ox feeding in an open valley between the river and a range of low hills. The group had split into two herds. In the distance to the south, surrounded by a herd of perhaps four hundred grazing caribou were fifteen or sixteen animals. Nearby were another thirty adults, most with small calves, of which fourteen adults and seven calves were sleeping or ruminating on the tundra.

The musk-ox's winter coats dragged on the ground, and close as I was, I still could not see legs or feet. But now I could see faces and the short, white, curving horns. The shaggy beasts moved slowly, deliberately. I didn't think them capable of fast action. But all at once a red fox appeared near the resting group and charged at a calf three times its size. At once the adults were up and crowding together, the calves seeking protection behind and beneath them. A defensive line formed quickly and the fox skipped away, obviously unafraid. Perhaps in play, perhaps in earnest, the fox had tested the musk-ox and was content to go in search of more reasonable prey.

Hours later the musk-ox dispersed into a loose herd that moved in and about hundreds of scattered caribou. Feeding, the two species ignored each other. The sun broke through the cloud cover and mottled the tundra in light and dark. Ground squirrels poked from their holes. Now and again ptarmigan flushed from willow thickets and plovers darted and bobbed on the sere plain. I was struck by the parallel between this scene and that which must have been common to the Western plains in the early 1800s. The northern tundra—a prairie really—supports a variety of life roughly analogous to the bison, antelope, prairie dogs, and sharp-tailed grouse that once abounded on the American prairie. In the distance the ubiquitous raven gossiped into the wind. Nowhere was the hand of man.

In the following days I followed the musk-ox into the foothills, where they sought the first green grass of spring. I stopped in the willows after they passed through and picked the fine underfur that clung to the branches wherever a musk-ox had stopped to scratch. I filled a large plastic bag with the rare and valuable *qiviut*. Full, the bag weighed but ounces.

It was time to leave the musk-ox and head downstream after the caribou. Near Itkilyarik Creek I saw an immature golden eagle feeding on the remains of an arctic fox. It was the second dead fox I'd seen. Rabies is common in arctic foxes, and I'd heard that sometimes even caribou contracted the disease after being bitten by a fox. I wondered what would become of the young eagle.

One sleep later and near the coast I approached a band of caribou. While still over a mile from the herd, I flushed a small calf from the brush. The bleating calf leaped up and trotted in wide circles around me. Oftentimes cows leave their calves sleeping on the tundra and feed some distance away, but this calf had been abandoned. I did not know what to do except to continue. Though I tried to dissuade it, the calf followed me. When I got within a quarter-mile of the main group, I climbed a low ridge, hoping the calf would follow and perhaps see the herd in the distance. To my delight it did just that and raced off to join the herd. I had no way of knowing whether its mother was in this group, but it was better off there than alone. Undoubtedly a lost calf would run up to a wolf in the same pathetic way it had latched onto me.

The days rolled into weeks—or so I calculated—and I began to wear out. My main rations, freeze-dried foods, were beginning to take a toll. Each day I felt more tired and listless. I covered ten miles or more a day but that would have been nothing had I been working on good food. I longed for fresh fruit and meat.

After days of snow and rain, of being, wet, cold, and hungry, I was content to relax away a warm, sunny afternoon. I lay on the tundra soaking up the sun. Soon the mosquitoes would hatch and swarm over the land, but now I enjoyed the still afternoon. Overhead a jet streaked high above the thin, scattered clouds—one of only a few I had seen or heard in the preceding days—on a polar route to Europe. I thought of the people in fine clothes that sat in that plane, impatient and bored, picking at a good, hot meal, perhaps enjoying a cold drink. My stomach growled at the image.

How those people would stare at me if I were suddenly thrust into their midst. Four weeks without a bath. But then, how out of place *they* would look if suddenly set down on the tundra. It was stunning to think that in a split second they traveled a distance that would take me days to cover on foot. I thought of the attractive attendants that must be serving the food. I remembered the stewardess on the Wien flight to Barter Island. The long legs in nylons, the tight black dress, the voluptuous chest, the long hair streaming down her back . . . I wanted the meal more.

I calculated that my time was up and started toward the rendezvous, a tiny grass flat on the bank of the Sadlerochit River where Walt Audi had agreed to pick me up. It would take two days for me to get there.

While plodding along, head down, happy the wind was keeping the mosquitoes at bay, I blundered on another abandoned caribou calf. The calf spooked from cover at a run and approached me, bleating most forlornly. I knelt down and the calf came running up to me and stopped five yards away. Its ribs showed plainly, and it looked emaciated. How long it had waited in the grass for its mother to return I did not know, but I did know that the nearest herd was probably ten or fifteen miles to the west.

I stood up and continued, the calf trotting a few yards behind. About a half-mile upriver the calf stopped following. Later, through the binoculars, I looked back and saw the calf staring toward the west. A grizzly was walking the ridge above the river. I turned upstream. I did not look back again.

FIVE

DALL SHEEP
Footprints in the Clouds

I

Gray smoke curls upward as flame gnaws the twig teepee that I shelter from the rain with my hands. As the fire takes hold, I add ever larger pieces of dry spruce. Later, when it's at its hottest, I'll use rain-dampened willow.

It has been raining hard all day. Usually it takes five hours to get this far into the mountains; today it has taken eight. The heavy runoff forced us out of the creekbed and onto the brushy sidehill. We fought alders most of the way, but several times we had to ford the swollen creek. At timberline we stopped in the last good place to build a fire.

I lean away from the smoke while hugging the fire as close as I dare. Back in the timber, Phil is changing into dry clothes. Soon I'll do the same, but just now, the fire, built streamside below a cutbank that reflects the heat, feels too good to leave. It is August 9, the day before the opening of sheep season.

Phil joins me. He fills the boil pot with creek water and sets it on a flat rock I've placed by the fire. While he tends the fire, I hunt dry clothes and set up the tent.

Under the spruce the rain slants down with lessened force. I look up at the mist-draped mountains and think of the sheep there. *We're each burdened with fifty-pound packs*, I think, *and there live the sheep, protected from the worst of the weather with nothing more than their birthright.* While pitching the tent, I picture the rams grazing through the clouds.

Later, sitting by the fire, I take off my boots and pour a cup of dirty water from each. After fishing out the soggy insoles, I pull off my socks and rub my white, wrinkled feet. A long-distance race, an infantry march, and a sheep hunt are the occasions when a person most appreciates the importance of healthy feet. In these circumstances a simple blister can be a catastrophe.

I stand with my back to the fire, steam rising from my pants as well as from my boots, now propped against the heat. As the warmth soaks in, the weariness fades and is replaced with faint exhilaration. The woodsmoke, the smell of timberline, and even the rain and fatigue, say it's sheep season.

Phil opens the plastic bag of instant coffee and spoons some into cups of boiled creekwater. We're playing a game with the weather, I tell him. Once the clouds lift, we might see sheep—probably rams—on the mountains on either side of us. Although I've seen sheep tracks in the bottoms, I add, it is unusual to see them straying very far from the protecting cliffs. I point ahead to where the drainage curves southward. We'll camp on the shore of the lake there and hunt the surrounding slopes and cirques.

I explain that these sheep have favored hangouts segregated by sex. The ewes and their lambs live in just two or three basins below the highest peaks; the rams, in small bands of five or six, though on occasion up to twenty, are elsewhere. Although the rams *seem* to prefer the drier slopes, I have been unable to see much difference in locations. Yet every year the ewes are in their places, the rams in theirs. It is an advantage to know this.

Phil goes to the tent and brings back bowls, spoons, and packages of freeze-dried meals. We have seven entrées to choose from. Just add boiling water, wait five minutes, and eat. We each open our packets—mine chili and beans, his turkey and noodles—and pour in the water. I wait a beat, then look up. Phil's puzzled look says: "This is dinner?"

Welcome Phil, to Ram Creek Gourmet Restaurant and Lodge.

Serving and eating this modest amount of food breaks the age-old rule of war and outfitting: an army marches on its stomach. But hell, did we come to hunt or to eat? Some outfitters are always talking about the food they serve, as if they were gourmet restaurateurs. Are Americans so pre-occupied with filets and desserts that they can't function for two weeks without steak and cake? Part of hunting is being in the country, getting wet and cold, working hard, and going a little hungry. It's part of learning a little of what the quarry knows well.

Phil tastes his meal and admits that it is good. He says his pack is already too heavy and can only imagine what it would have been like before the advent of dehydrated foods.

We spend a quiet evening by the fire watching both the flames and the lowering clouds. Around nine o'clock the rain turns to snow. At nine-thirty we crawl in the tent. I fall asleep to the wind in the trees.

Silence rouses me. I sit up and pull back the tent flap. The ground is covered with a snow that continues to fall. It is five-thirty, the usual time to get up, but instead I lie back down.

At eight I am again awakened, but this time by a rising wind. I dress and leave the tent. The storm has passed and the sun has broken through. While Phil collects wood, I start the fire.

By noon, the clouds are all but gone and the snow is melting fast. By early afternoon we are well up the canyon, both of us finding forgotten muscles. A mile above the campsite the alders end, and we are finally able to hike open tundra. I am glad to quit the brush, but wet tundra, covered as it is with grass tussocks that twist underfoot, makes easy walking impossible. Snow patches hide many pitfalls, and at best we lurch along under our packs like drunken ducks.

Halfway to the lake we take a break on a dry knob. We snack on gorp, sausage, and cheese, washed down with powdered orange drink. The white-on-black mountains rear against an azure sky dappled with cumulus. A raven circles above a distant ridge; ptarmigan chatter in the brush across the canyon. We don't see any sheep.

Two hours later we are at the lake and setting up camp by its outlet, where multitudes of grayling jump for insects. The patchy snow turns to ice as the sun dips behind the peaks.

Over dinner Phil says that a good tent with a waterproof fly and a dependable stove are absolute musts for a trip into the high country. I agree. There's precious little firewood here, and hypothermia conditions are an alpine norm. A dry tent and hot liquids can save a life.

The next morning we rise at five to frost on the tent. It's painful putting on stiff boots. In a half-hour we are out of camp and climbing. In our packs we each carry raingear, extra clothes, poly bottles of water, and food. In addition I have the spotting scope, pack saw, and two meat sacks. We wear binoculars around our necks.

We angle up a long ridge heading for the northern rim of the canyon. It has always seemed useless to me to attempt to spot sheep from below, as easily hidden as they are by the natural folds and lines of this standing-on-end country. I prefer to climb up high and look in all directions. The climbing is also part of why we are here.

The first few hundred feet of the climb are almost painful. Early morning muscles, already strained by two days of backpacking, seem unwilling to stretch out and relax. To hurry the process, I push myself. My lungs gulp fresh air. On a little knob I stop to rest and look over the country. Phil is right behind me. Almost as one we raise our binoculars.

Under the subdued light of the overcast, sheep will be easier to spot. Contrary to the usual belief, I know these white sheep are not all that easy to locate. The sun's glare on the slopes can hide a band of sheep—even those standing in the open—and make white rocks stand out and look like sheep. Often, spotting rams is merely a matter of waiting for the angle of light to change. Under the right conditions, a white sheep on a green background *can* be seen by the naked eye, even on a mountain miles away. Seldom, however, are conditions ideal.

I glass the immediate slopes and cirques but see nothing. The broken snow makes our task doubly difficult. With careful scanning, in time, I expect to see both sheep and their tracks.

Looking down, I trace the course of the creek as it winds across open tundra toward the dark green of timberline. I never can believe it takes almost five hours to hike that seemingly short distance. The lake is always such a compelling destination. It nestles at the head of the drainage in a cirque carved in millennia past by a great glacier, now just a tiny relic below the tallest peak. In early season, rams can often be found nearby.

When we start upward again, it's warm enough for snowmelt. Soon we're clambering over boulders covered with a black lichen that resembles burned corn flakes. When dry, these corn flakes crackle and break under foot; when wet, they are slimy and dangerous. Between the boulders are holes big enough to swallow a leg, or a whole person. From below comes the echo of running water. The fading snow hides many crevices, making risk the name of the game. Either of us could twist an ankle or take a fall. A broken leg could threaten life.

Two thirds of the way up the mountain, I finally reach second gear. My legs feel good, and I move at an easy, fast pace. I'm startled when I look back and see Phil lagging behind. Stepping from one rock to another, some teetering beneath my feet, I climb hard to a huge boulder a few yards ahead. There I dump my pack and wait for Phil. I never sit down when I stop for a break—I like to stand and stretch. Sometimes, when I'm really tired, it's too much of a mental free-for-all to get back up; I sit or recline only when I need to steady the binoculars or spotting scope.

Just as Phil reaches me, I locate tracks in the snow and then four white spots on the gray rock of the opposite ridgeline. In his laconic way Phil says nothing when I point out the sheep. Instead he takes his glasses out from under his shirt and peers across canyon at the first mountain sheep he's ever seen.

"Rams," I predict, without seeing horns. Phil nods his head. I get out the spotting scope, steady it on the pack, and with the aid of 35X magnification, see horns silhouetted against cloud.

Careful not to bump the scope, I move away and invite Phil to take a look. I watch his face as he sees his first white ram. He almost whistles. I picture the lemon-yellow, full-curl horns sweeping past the white faces and around the jewel eyes; the dirt- and grass-stained rumps and flanks. I can almost smell their peculiar musky scent.

Through my binoculars I watch the rams feeding along the ridge toward the head of the canyon.

"They're beautiful," says Phil. "Thin lower legs like antelope but with powerful upper bodies. They look fast."

I describe their speed going uphill and across rocky slopes. When pressed, or going downhill, they cover fifteen feet a jump.

"Now that I know where to look I can see them with my unaided eye," he says. "Can they see us?"

"About twenty minutes ago they knew you wore Levi's and a cowboy shirt, and had less hair than I do."

Phil laughs at my exaggeration. Sheep do have phenomenal visual acuity. At this distance the rams won't run off, but I don't doubt they've seen us. In fact, even as I watch, one looks up and stares in our direction. I imagine he's reading the label on my binoculars.

I have to take the spotting scope away from Phil to get him to move on. Those four will be there another day.

An hour later we stop just below the crest of the ridge where two ravens hover in the updrafts howling over the rocky summit. I look back in dismay to see the opposite ridge draped in clouds. In all directions the sky is lowering and I can almost smell rain. One front with snow and cold has passed; another has arrived, carrying rain.

I rummage through my pack for my long john top, wool shirt, vest, down jacket, watch cap, and gloves. I strip off my wet T-shirt and dress hurriedly. Phil does the same. *Oh, for a shaft of warm sunlight!*

Phil waits by the packs while I sneak ahead, binoculars in one hand, spotting scope in the other. I crawl the last few feet to the crest, excited as always to solve the riddle of what's over the next ridge. For a long moment I lie motionless. Long ago I walked to a crest like this and looked straight into the face of a ram lying not thirty feet away. All I could do was watch as it ran off. Since then I've been more careful.

With chin on crossed hands, I study the familiar north-facing basin, looking for movement more than anything else. Next I use my binoculars to study every dent and cliff in the bowl. Once I saw eleven rams hidden here, all but two of them legal. This time around I locate six white specks just below the clouds descending the eastern rim. With the scope I identify them as rams. Before I can beckon to Phil, they are hidden in the clouds that fifteen minutes later engulf us.

We decide to wait it out, hoping the clouds will lift. We alternately sit, stand, jump, and finally run in place. Even with my outerwear on, exercise can't keep the chill at bay. Three hours pass and when it begins to sprinkle, we give up. Halfway down the mountain we emerge from the clouds.

Going down is harder than going up. The rain on slush-covered rocks makes each step precarious; we move like old men with bad knees. By late afternoon we make it back to the coffee. *Ah, Big Ram Creek Gourmet Restaurant and Lodge.*

The next three days follow the same pattern. We rise early to overcast skies, make a long hard climb to the top, spot sheep, lose them in descending clouds, return to camp in the rain. Another day, however, is different. It sleets on us at the summit. *August. Summer north of the Arctic Circle.*

The seventh day of the ten-day hunt dawns under light rain. It takes real effort to get out of the warm bag and into damp clothes. Time is running out, and despite the weather we've got to keep trying.

"Have the cook make French toast and eggs," comes the voice from a hole in the mummy bag next to me.

In short order I hand out instant coffee and granola spiced with fresh blueberries. "Here ya' go. Over easy and lots of syrup."

Despite the rain, this day seems better. The clouds are high and we can see the tops of the peaks again. From camp I glass all the slopes and ridges to the south and west. Two miles downstream I spot two white specks, which focus in the scope as a very large full-curl ram accompanied by a half-curl.

The stalk begins from the tent. The rams command a view of the entire valley from the end of the lake to a point three miles down canyon. We have but one option: hug the extreme north side of the valley until out of sight downstream and hope the rams will not react to our distant passing.

An hour later we are hidden from the sheep by the high flank of the mountain. The last time we saw them, they had stopped watching us and had returned to grazing. On the hard-hunted sheep ranges to the south the rams would have been long gone. We can only hope these two haven't spooked.

Once on the steep slope I rapidly overheat in my plastic cocoon so I stop to strip off my raincoat. Rain or sweat, it's all the same. Phil follows my lead. While he pulls off his raingear, I eye the bow and arrows he's laid on the ground. With a rifle hunter, I'd predict that we still have an excellent chance to kill a sheep, but an archery hunt is different. At the outset we needed all the time available to us, several different opportunities for a stalk, plus a dash of luck. Already three fourths of the hunt is over and we've not stalked a single sheep.

The hard work combined with the cold and damp have exacted a toll. The climb is slow and exhausting. The sodden ground gives way and often I slide back two steps for every one forward. More than once we slip to our knees. Instead of the fast pace of the first few days, I now climb a few feet, stop to blow, climb some more, then rest again. Despite knowing that one sunny day would dispel this lethargy, I cannot now muster more vigor.

Just below the rim of the basin we stop and shuck our packs. It's raining harder and I pull out my raincoat. With the inside as wet as the outside I put it on only as a gesture. Phil just wipes his brow with a soiled red bandana and grins his lopsided grin.

We creep to the rim together and peer over. Low scud swirls over the rocks, blotting visibility. For a brief minute or two I see the sheep at the head of the bowl. The one ram carries a huge set of horns. A few minutes later they vanish in the opaque clouds.

Hours later, after another futile wait, we give up and climb down. The fog extends right down to the creek bottom. It seems a mocking insult.

The next day I awake to silence and bright sun. I wriggle out of my bag and crawl to the door. Blue sky. *No rain!* Phil, his mustache curled into its own smile, crawls out of the tent right behind me. In moments we have everything we own laid out on the rocks to dry. Soon we are drinking coffee and enjoying the heat.

Two hours later, feeling guilty for lingering in camp, we again head up the first ridge we'd climbed. Partway up we look across canyon and see what probably are the same four rams we spotted the first day. Immediately we start down. Soon we walk past the tent, wade the outlet stream (cold water is now routine), and start up the steep pitch.

I plan to circle behind the ridge and come out in a position above where we last saw the rams. Halfway there, an up-canyon wind obliterates Plan A. Instead we head straight for the top.

The climb goes well and we seldom pause. The sunshine and renewed hope make the difference. Phil never lags yet neither seems in a hurry to pass. Once I hang out my tongue like a tired greyhound. So much for the half-man, half–mountain goat guide mystique.

Halfway to the summit the wind begins to switch. We fear the rams have already scented us and will be gone before we see them.

Like so many other times in the preceding days, we creep to the edge, half expecting clouds or vacant real estate. Instead, the rams are perched on a moraine in the middle of the basin, seemingly doing little more than soaking up the sun. We'd need a great deal of luck just to get within five hundred yards of them, which isn't even good rifle range. Long-range shooting is an accepted part of sheep hunting, a part I don't like. Clean-killing shots at long range are hard to make. Besides, the value of an animal is reduced when it is viewed through a rifle scope at long range. I try to get my rifle hunters within at least two hundred yards of a ram. In contrast, a bowhunt depends on a stalk to close range. Phil says anything over forty yards is too far.

We hunker down to wait. In early afternoon the rams get up and start to feed slowly uphill. One by one they climb out of the bowl and disappear over the ridge. When the last ram goes out of sight, we jump up, grab our packs and hurry up the ridge, staying well below the skyline. Ignoring protesting muscles, I force myself into a hurried walk. At the top, knowing the rams could be anywhere, we slow to a cautious pace.

I step from rock to rock as quietly as I can, Phil right behind me. The small sounds of our packs, clothes, and footfalls, seem loud in the tense expectation. A slight movement downhill stops us in our tracks, but it is only a weasel dodging in and out of the rocks. I feel good about seeing it; we are attuned.

It takes a long time to reach the point where the rams exited the cirque. We hide in the rocks there and glass the open slope. Nothing. The rams must be in the one spot we cannot look into, a pasturage below a humped shoulder of the mountain. The only way to find out is to climb down and see.

I whisper out our options. Once committed to descending the slope, we'll be without cover. We discuss our next move. Finally Phil points downhill: *Let's go.*

We start down with infinite care, well aware that the rams could be hidden in an unseen depression or behind a rockpile. The squirrelly wind makes me nervous. Even though mountain sheep pay little attention to noise—the mountains a noisy world of wind, falling rock and water—they do heed their sense of smell. It takes us twenty minutes to descend to a point slightly above the supposed hiding place. Phil helps me out of my pack and I help him out of his. We crawl to the edge.

About two hundred yards away lies a lone ram with its back to us. I cannot see the other three rams. I steady the scope on a rock and focus in. This one has a nice but not exceptional set of horns. Although I can't see all the annual rings on the horns, I guess him to be eight to ten years old. After a long look, I whisper the distance to Phil as he takes over the scope. I expect him to show some excitement but all I see is that small smile.

While he studies the ram, I look in vain for the others. The wind now is to our advantage, but unless we see the other rams, the stalk looks risky.

After an inordinate length of time behind the scope, Phil backs away. He signals me to lean close. He whispers that he thinks he can make the stalk but is worried about the other rams. Should we wait and try again tomorrow? I remind him that we have only one more day to hunt and the weather can change quickly.

Phil studies the ram and intervening terrain. He whispers that this sight alone has made the long trip, the bad weather, and my cooking all worthwhile.

The ram makes our decision for us. He gets up, stretches, and strolls over the edge and out of sight. If Phil hurries to the lip of the hill, he can perhaps get a shot. Without prompting he's up and moving, his bow in one hand, an arrow in the other. I watch as he hurries downhill and then out across the flat. If that ram or another comes back over the brow, the jig is up. There'll be no second chance.

Near where the ram disappeared, Phil pauses to nock an arrow. In a crouch he moves forward in exaggerated slow motion. Suddenly he stops and lowers his head. It is obvious he's seen something. He bends deeper and creeps closer. He stops, rises a little, then freezes. Turned to stone. It is maddening not to see what is happening. I know the ram, or rams, must be staring back at him. I wonder how far they are, if he'll get a shot, if he'll become one of only about two dozen people ever to kill a Dall ram with an arrow.

Finally he straightens and draws the bow. At full draw he takes two steps forward, stops, aims, and releases the arrow. It zings over the ridge. He grabs for another arrow mounted in the bow quiver. He nocks that one, again raises the bow, aims, and releases. I see it whistle over the ridge in the same path as the first.

Phil runs out of sight over the ridge. I hurry after him. From where he'd stood, I see at a distance three rams running hard toward the west. A fourth soon races into sight behind them.

A few moments later Phil joins me to watch the white specks disappear in the distance. He shakes his head.

"Just blew it," he says. "Looked over and the ram was looking right back at me. I knew he could only see the top of my head and so waited him out. As soon as he looked away, I took my shot. The wind is blowing crossways here. My first shot was going perfect, then I saw the wind catch it and it started to sail, skipped off his horn."

He holds out an arrow and points to the dent in the aluminum.

"He just swapped ends and looked downhill. He must have thought whatever hit him was down there. I tried to compensate for the wind with my second shot but it went straight over his back. That time he knew it was me. I didn't see the other rams until he bolted. They were right below him.

"Two misses at thirty-five yards."

We search for the second arrow. Phil finds it some distance downhill, the broadhead smashed on the rocks. We head back to our packs, then continue up to the top. We sit for a while, glassing the peaks and basins. For the first time we can see all the way north to Gates of the Arctic. Three groups of sheep, all too far to identify, are feeding within a few hours' climb from camp. Except for some clouds to the south, the sky is clear in all directions and holds promise for tomorrow.

We arrive at camp in twilight. Over dinner we sit in silence and watch grayling dimpling the lake. The wind off the water carries the hawk bite of autumn.

In the tent later, when the shadows are full, and long after I thought he was asleep, Phil makes one last comment.

"One more day. Hope it's a good one," he says, "but if not, I've got my memories." He doesn't sound disappointed.

Sometime in the night I stir to hard rain on the tent. By morning it has turned to snow.

II

John Hewitt guided sheep hunters with me for parts of five years. Together we were low-comedy confederates, sharing a humor rooted in a traditional Middle America upbringing. I'm certain the majority of the hunters we put through boot camp thought we were loons. If Hewitt had a motto, it must have been, *Always be comic in a tragedy.*

Neither of us ever won any awards for being well dressed. His mother once asked if I saved all my old clothes for hunting. I told her I didn't have any old clothes.

Hewitt always dressed practically, in layers. Like the Inuit, he had a remarkable tolerance for cold weather; he commonly was more comfortable in just his brown cotton T-shirt than his hunter was in a wool shirt and down jacket. Even in cold weather he wore not a parka but a windbreaker, usually a hooded nylon rain jacket, over a light flannel shirt and a medium wool shirt. Cloth work gloves came out when it turned cold, and he carried wool glove liners in case it got bitter.

He wore loose-fitting Levi's held up with loggers' suspenders, and covered his Marine Corps haircut—basic skinhead—with a blue watch cap. His clothing seemed to say, "knowledge, ability is power; appearance, nothing."

On many of our sheep hunts, because much of the ground was wet, Hewitt preferred Vietnam-style jungle boots with lug soles. Those boots were a constant reminder of an important chapter in his life. He looks so young for his age, 44 in 1989, that it's hard to recall how much he's been through. Somewhere I have a picture of him holding a nice catfish. He's wearing jeans, T-shirt, and a mangled straw hat. The car behind him has Kansas plates. The heck of it is, the picture could have been taken yesterday. Oh, perhaps in the picture he's a little thinner and has more hair, though you can't tell because of the hat, but there's not much difference. The inscription reveals that it was taken well over twenty years ago.

The first time we met, I thought him to be eighteen. I was ten years off—we were the same age. I was no less amazed to find out he had a graduate degree in English and was an accomplished—no, outstanding—writer of hunting and fishing short stories. At times he so mangled the English language with *ain'ts*, double negatives and profanity worthy of the Marines that I wondered how short-circuited the system must have been to award him a degree of any kind, let alone an advanced one.

But every now and again, most often in mixed company, he'd shift idioms: his grammer would become flawless, his slight drawl disappear, his vocabulary expand. In one of the stories he wrote about himself, he spoke of a time when "one wondered how one could ever be so foolish as to pursue anything in life besides the study of literature." He could quote from Hemingway, Ruark, Faulkner, Shakespeare, Byron, and most often, Frost and Whitman. His ability to quote lengthy sections of poetry and recall events from his childhood still astounds me.

A varied background and astonishing memory made Hewitt a formidable raconteur. He could spin detailed, humorous stories about hunting, old flames, academia, the military, most any topic. He could entertain laborer or executive, be earthy or erudite. With Hewitt around I had the luxury in the evening of just listening. Once, I looked across the smoky fire and saw more than one man talking. Since before recorded history, hunters sitting around campfires have been enthralled by storytellers. In central Asia, the Kirghiz people still revere storytellers, some of whom can recite three-hour epics of hunting on the steppes. John would be a natural.

No matter how grim the circumstance, Hewitt found something funny about it, and his grin more than once cheered me. That grin, however, hid a core of grief and pain. Again he seemed like the Inuit, who retreat into a smile, a mask of inscrutable affability, the smile of the outsider.

Hewitt had been in the Marine Corps. He'd been a second lieutenant during the Vietnam War. Despite his own suffering, he seemed unaffected by the desensitizing and confusing experiences of that tragic conflict. He accepted his misfortune, his family's loss, and his experience with a straightforward equanamity. Unlike some veterans, he spoke of the Marine Corps with undisguised pride and respect, and said he would do the same things over again, given the opportunity.

On August 7, 1968, with eleven months' time in service and only seven days in Vietnam, near Danang, he was seriously wounded by a hand grenade of Chinese origin. Doctors removed shrapnel, wood, and bone from Hewitt's brain, replaced the blood he'd lost through a severed temporal artery, and did what they could with the hole through his lower leg. From Vietnam he was flown to a hospital in Japan. There, a severe infection developed, and several more cleansing operations by neurosurgeons were necessary. Things were, in his words, "nip and tuck there for a while." When he finally was capable of calling home to reassure his parents, he said, "Hi, Mom. I guess I'll be home for duck season." He spent half a year in hospitals, undergoing physical therapy.

Two years later, his twin brother, Thomas, a captain commanding a company with the 101st Airborne, was killed by a rifle-propelled grenade near Khe Sahn.

Even-tempered and cheery, John made a great assistant guide. The hunters took to him like to a new retriever found under the Christmas tree. Hewitt said he'd title his memoirs, *I Never Met a Man I Didn't Like for Ten or Fourteen Days.*

I don't know how many generations in Hewitt's lineage were hunters, but it would be surprising to find mention of a male who wasn't. In his family the values of one generation were passed to the next. He spoke of hunts with Dad and Gramps. When his first child, Katherine, was six, he outfitted her in camouflage and took her in the canoe to hunt ducks. Hunting as heritage. Once, when we spoke about political efforts to ban guns and hunting, he said, "It might be right in some places, but it wouldn't be right for me."

Having hunted all his life, he was a consummate outdoorsman, and I never worried about a hunter entrusted to his care. He wasn't the best judge of sheep heads, nor the most avid sheep hunter, but he knew the country.

His goal in sheep hunting was to bring back not the biggest sheep but a satisfied hunter, with as few close calls in the process as possible. If a hunter would be happy with a handsome ram of less-than-record stature, encountered on the second day of a ten-day hunt, you'd never hear Hewitt say, "I'm sure if we're patient we can find a bigger one." Rather, he'd get his man to within comfortable rifle shot of the sheep by the safest and surest route, give him time to settle down after the stalk, spot his shot for him, and meticulously cape and butcher the result. It is worth noting that in the years he worked with me, no hunter assigned to him ever used more than one cartridge on a sheep hunt, and Hewitt himself used none.

From Hewitt I learned something about outdoor cookery, how to get the coals and the heat just right, and how to slice meat for quick, even cooking. I learned a lot about meat care. I'd had plenty of training in caring for hides and capes, but woefully little with butchering—boning, turning chunks into roasts, steaks, and chops. He was expert.

No matter how hard the task at hand, or how much work involved, he always did more than his share. I remember one hunt when both of our hunters killed nice rams on the same day. When it came time to pack out, I stuffed my pack with gear and meat but there was still some left over. We discussed making relays to get everything out, but in the end, Hewitt heaped everything he could into his pack and tied the rest on top. It was all he could do to stand up under the load. Without one word of complaint, he headed down canyon.

Hewitt was a true subsistence hunter. Ptarmigan, mallards, pheasant, grayling, salmon, trout—a huge portion of all that crossed his table was caught, shot, or grown in his garden. He seldom hunted large animals but avidly hunted ducks, ptarmigan, and grouse. Each autumn he went south to hunt pheasants and ducks in his native Kansas. When he looked at an animal, he did not first comment on its beauty or size, or that he wanted to shoot it, but that he bet it would be *"good to eat."*

When I first met him, his routine was to work construction jobs in winter, and guide and hunt in the fall. His guiding career came to an abrupt end when he married Mary Coote and settled into raising a family. He surprised none of his close friends when he knuckled down to the task of building a quality home and working in construction and the oil fields. There remained, in this industrious new direction his life took, however, one thing unchanged; he still set aside two months after the leaves went off for his own hunting.

Through the reality of war, physical pain, bereavement from the loss of a brother, divorce, and the usual array of human travail, Hewitt's world always looked all right to him in October when viewed over a shotgun. I have heard him say, on a dozen occasions, by campfires and on frosty mornings after the tundra has turned colors, with nothing to look forward to but the drudgery of a dawn-to-dusk hike under a cruelly heavy pack, "After all, a guy is damn lucky to be here, ain't he?"

III

Just as bears follow distinct trails used generation after generation, paw print upon paw print, mountain sheep use routes etched across cliffs and slopes by the passing of uncounted hooves. Some trails are temporary tracings across loose sand and gravel; others are permanent toeholds worn into near-perpendicular rock.

Most sheep trails follow the line of least resistance, winding and detouring around boulders, cliffs, and precipices. They cross rock, gravel, sand, snow, and grass. Many routes are not permanent but ever-changing, perhaps day by day, as even the mountains themselves change. Some are nothing more than scrapings on boulders that are spanned with leaps. As indistinct as these paths may appear to human eyes, they are obvious to their users.

Whether mountain sheep trails are passable for human beings depends in part on terrain, local climate, and geologic composition, not to mention the climber's limitations and inclinations. Often what is above the trail may come tumbling down on it; what's below it for the climber to tumble into may also have some bearing on suitability. Trails across scree slopes can be difficult to traverse because each step sets the detritus in motion. It takes strength and effort to work quickly across to more solid footing.

It's the trails across cliffs that are most unsuitable for people. Some paths on solid rock are easy to follow, though not recommended for acrophobics. The view often is unparalleled, the footholds solid and sure. I've gotten myself into trouble edging along cliffs where I've had to play mind games to keep from looking down. With growing apprehension I've boot-tipped along until the trail faded into nothing. Almost to where I could neither go forward or back, I've clutched at fingerholds, thinking, *to hell with this—I'm scouting sheep, not mountain climbing!* and begun a painful, exhausting reverse.

Often I've crept along some precarious trail and come on a sheep bed tucked into a ledge. I find handfuls of dried, raisin-sized pellets, tufts of hair clinging to the rocks, and the pungent aroma of musk and urine. The beds always look the same, almost like nests. In the dust there are often tracks and an impression of the sheep's body. I've rested in many of them, reveling in the view.

The trails along ridgetops afford easy walking and great views of the canyons and ridges on either side. Often these higher trails lead to promontories commanding tremendous sweeps of country. I've found clusters of beds around these favored lookouts, where a band of resting sheep can detect movement from any quadrant.

One warm summer's day on Sheep Mountain I sat with seven rams bedded on a slope in the shade of a steep cliff. It was humbling to be on that mountainside within a few feet of those rams, watching them ruminate and doze away the day. I sat so close I could hear their stomachs rumbling and their deep sighs as they drifted in and out of sleep. I also could look beyond them to the glaciered spires and emerald slopes of the Chugach Mountains.

Dall sheep are light sleepers and never blank out for lengthy periods. At the slightest disturbance their eyes snap open to check for enemies. (The pattern's much the same for a ram or a robin.) A sheep relaxes with one foreleg extended, otherwise the front quarters are curled underneath ready for flight. Sometimes a weary ram will put its chin on the ground, or lay its head to the side to rest on one horn. With horns and skull nearing thirty-five pounds, it's a rest well-earned.

Rams were once thought to post sentinels when they sleep, so that one ram would always be alert to warn of danger. Rams do lie facing in all directions, but apparently not because of some duty roster for visual surveillance. Rather they seek to avoid direct eye contact with one another. Since sheep are fitful sleepers, and since they tend to face in varied directions, ram bands *are* difficult to sneak up on, but not because one sheep is relegated to guard duty.

Some trails lead to mineral licks—"salt licks," as they are called. Mountain sheep crave the rich soils and may travel many miles to reach them. Some scientists believe sodium is the lure. Others suggest that sheep eat the mud not for "salt," but because the ingestion of the calcium- and magnesium-rich soils is needed to balance the potassium from plants. Still others suspect that the clay soil may in itself help rid the digestive system of internal parasites.

Near some of these places, like the Dry Creek lick in the Alaska Range east of Wood River, market hunters built stone blinds and shot down whole herds, young and old, ram and ewe. Piles of rifle casings, testament to the efficiency of the technique, can still be found in these blinds.

Some Native hunters hid in ambush along sheep trails. Rock cairns occasionally were built in human shape to deflect sheep into the ambush. Because of the difficulty involved in mountain hunting, and the lack of predictable success, sheep were not a primary food source, even for mountain people. The few killed were highly prized; the skins were used for clothing, and ram horns made into unique ladles.

Today, villagers of Kaktovik, a small Inuit community on Barter Island at the edge of the polar ice cap, travel south each winter across the arctic plain to camps in the Brooks Range. There they hunt sheep, trap arctic fox, and fish for char in open pools along the otherwise frozen rivers. The Brooks Range offers refuge from the monotony of the wind-raked island, and sheep meat's a welcome addition to their diet.

Human beings are not the only ones to utilize sheep trails. Once in the Chugach Mountains, after a brutal day and a half of struggling up from the Matanuska River through alder jungles, a companion and I gained the summit of a fifty-six-hundred-foot hogback. Two bull moose, their antlers overhanging the edge, were single-filing down the trail ahead of us.

In the mountains I've also encountered grizzlies, or their diggings and tracks. Just as sheep trails are not designed for people, bears seldom keep to them for long unless they lead to marmot or squirrel colonies. Once on Sheep Mountain, a ram I had been photographing strolled to the edge of the ridge and looked down. Something frightened him, and he led the band away in panicked flight. I walked to the edge, expecting to see climbers, but instead saw a grizzly digging out a squirrel a few yards away. I ducked down and bailed off the opposite side of the ridge, skiing the loose sand and gravel slope to the bottom.

Wolves and coyotes kill sheep when they can. Twice I have seen wolverines stalking bands of lambs and ewes. Biologist Lyman Nichols found evidence that a black bear had killed a sheep. Just after the turn of the century, Charles Sheldon reported finding a lynx-killed sheep. In Denali Park in the mid-1980s, a biologist found a ram killed by a lynx. These both must be considered rare occurrences.

Predators stalk these mountain trails in search of easy prey. Healthy sheep can usually elude predators but the alpine exacts a harsh toll. A fall, or even a minor injury, means lingering death. A sheep with a broken leg starves or falls victim to its enemies.

In the spring, ewes retreat to isolated cliffs to bear their young. They must remain alert not only for coyotes and wolves but also for golden eagles. Imperfect animals will soon be weeded out. Near a salt lick, I once saw a lamb dragging a deformed hindleg. Another time I saw a tiny lamb, just half the size of the others playing around it, lying motionless by a stunted willow. I thought it dead, but an approaching ewe called and it stirred. When the lamb struggled to its feet, I saw raw intestine beneath its tail. The ewe attempted to suckle her starving lamb but it collapsed. She sniffed the lamb's wound, then started away. When the lamb did not follow, she returned and roughly pawed it. Another ewe also sniffed and pawed the lamb's wound. By late afternoon the entire band had fed out from the canyon, leaving the injured lamb alone.

One spring, near Wiseman, I climbed a narrow avalanche chute toward a ridgeline from which I hoped to spot some rams. Partway up I came upon piles of hair and bones, then the skull and horns of two rams. I recognized the horns of one of them as those of a ram I'd seen the summer before. It was apparent they'd died in a snow slide. Perhaps wolves, foxes, and wolverines had shared the meat. Once I would have considered myself fortunate with such a find and packed home the skulls. Now, I set them together on a flat spot. I arranged them as if looking out over the mountains and the river shining silver in the sun, then walked away.

In Denali Park in September 1981, I took two friends up to visit some rams on a slope high above the Savage River. We watched one ram dance across a rock cliff. I have a photograph of him with only one hoof on the rock, his other three in midair.

Just as we were leaving, we noticed several ewes and lambs climbing upward from the heavy alders below. One lamb appeared injured, all four legs bathed in blood from the knees down. We got a close look when the whole band filed by us and I made several pictures. Not only were the lamb's legs bloody but its mouth and nostrils, as well as the joints above the hooves, were swollen with black lesions. We guessed it suffered from contagious ecthyma. A few years before, an outbreak of the disease in a captive herd of musk-ox and Dall sheep set off fears of a catastrophic zoodemic in Dall sheep, mountain goats, and caribou. Any time a disease or parasite is introduced into a wildlife population, the stage is set for catastrophe. In the Lower Forty-Eight and Canada, parasites and diseases transmitted from domestic stocks, and the destruction of winter range, have reduced mountain sheep to remnant and relict herds.

Although the exact source of the ecthyma was never identified, fingers pointed toward domestic sheep and goats, the major domestic animal reservoirs of the disease. Investigators eventually found traces of the disease in blood serum samples from wild goats and sheep in many parts of Alaska. It turned out that the disease was not new and that natural immunities had developed.

While watching the diseased lamb, we heard noise in the brush behind us and turned, expecting to see other sheep. Out of the alders stepped a grizzly, its nose to the ground like a bloodhound. We backed away but it was apparent that the bear had picked up the blood scent and would not be deterred. We could only stand and watch as the bear reached the bloody trail. Instead of turning uphill toward the lamb and us, it turned downhill and raced off on the backtrail. As soon as the thundering of three human hearts quieted, we hurried away.

For some prey species, predation is the controlling factor; for sheep populations, it is winter range and winter weather conditions. Wolves are the sheep's main predator, but many biologists doubt that wolves can control a sheep population directly. If severe snows or ice weaken sheep and make them easier prey, or force them out of escape terrain, then wolves *may* become the direct controlling factor.

Although spring lambs look frail, within two or three days of birth they can follow their mothers through the roughest terrain. During the first days of their lives, which may last thirteen to fourteen years at best, lambs seldom stray very far from their mothers. Later on, lambs form nursery groups, sometimes watched over by a ewe. They play on slopes and pas-

tures covered with mountain avens, moss campion, and scarlet plume.
With all the joy of health and new life, they jump and twist in midair and
chase each other over slab-sided cliffs. The games that constitute their
physical and social education take them where squirrels chirp from their
burrows, where marmots and pikas whistle in the rocks, where rock ptarmigan guard tundra kingdoms and ravens taunt the wind.

Being herd animals, the lambs soon learn to read their companions'
body language. A stiff, head-up pose attracts attention and sets all the sheep
on guard. When one sheep runs, they all run.

A year after their birth, usually during May and early June, when the
ewes again lamb, young males join bachelor bands; females stay in the same
group as their mothers, perhaps throughout life. Through this association
young sheep learn the trails and routes to and from winter and summer
range, as well as survival strategies. In Denali Park I've seen groups of
sheep well out on Polychrome Flats, and elsewhere, as they navigate the
dangerous flatlands between the outer and inner ranges, winter and
summer range.

Trails are the sheep's thumbprint on the land, the only scars of their
passing. I've flown and hiked over the Takoshas and Ray Mountains and
looked in vain for sheep or their trails. Without dollops of white sheep,
these mountains seem so empty.

One exploration in the Alaska Range led me along a sheep trail to
where a north-flowing river plunged through a narrow gorge. The wind
blew so hard through this natural venturi that I had difficulty standing. In
fact, when I was rounding the last boulder, the head-on blast staggered me
a few steps. I pushed forward and leaned into the wind, my arms out-
stretched like a bird, and would have fallen flat on my face if it had ceased.
I wanted to give a raven cry, *Caw! Caw!*

Another time, in the Brooks Range, I followed a trail slicing up off Poss
Mountain, hoping it would lead me to a particular ram. The trail went
along the knife-edge and I worked hard to follow it. But as I climbed
upward, I moved faster, exhilarated by the vistas and the fresh new air.
Higher and higher I climbed until my focus, my goal, became not ram's
horns, but the pinnacle daggering into the sky. The trail petered out. I
studied the final spire and picked out a route. Jamming feet and hands into
cracks in the rock, I climbed to the very top. I'd hoped for a pleasant stay
there, with a chance to enjoy the country to the north and east, but the
wind on sweat-soaked clothes was too much. Just as I thought to climb

down, I noticed a depression on the off side of the pinnacle. A sheep bed!

At once I lowered myself down to the hollow, gouged out just big enough for a sheep. I sat down in the bed amid the hair and droppings. It was calm and sheltered, and heat radiated from the sun-splashed rock that protected it on three sides—the warmest place I'd been in two weeks. The open side dropped off sharply and it seemed probable that the sheep that used this bed jumped down into it, just as I had.

Here was a perfect haven. Only a good climber, sheep or human, could reach this place. Nothing could approach unseen from below.

I sat there a long time, looking out over the summits stretching into the distance, down into the valley below where a mile-long lake sparkled like a tiny dewdrop, southwest to cumulous clouds puffing into the sky. I thought of the ram I had hunted—for surely this was his bed, his secret hideaway. He must have come here in some time of danger. No chance trail or pasturage would have led him here. I could picture him here in this spot, looking out at the world below, ears perked for the sound of falling rock. I also knew that I'd never come here hunting him.

IV

Mountain sheep adjust to human contact more readily than perhaps any other species of game. In Chugach State Park and Denali National Park, for example, Dall sheep allow people to approach to close range. In contrast, where they are hunted, human beings seem to cause greater alarm than enemies like wolves or bears. One glimpse of a person, even at a great distance, is sometimes enough to trigger flight. Some sheep use the terrain like magicians. I've seen many rams on cliffs above crevassed glaciers, places only eagles could approach. One ram, when spooked, escaped into a labyrinth of caves above a scree slope.

Long after I stopped guiding for most animals, I continued to hunt sheep. Having mastered the elementary skills, I lost the desire to kill but still found fascination in the hunt and stalk. There's just no such thing as an easy sheep hunt. Moose and bears have been shot in the middle of the road, or even inside towns, but not rams. It takes perseverance and honest work just to enter sheep country, let alone find and kill one. On a backpack hunt that may cover thirty-five miles, it would not be an exaggeration to say the stalk begins with the first step.

The area I hunted was relatively inaccessible, and I saw little change in the sheep population from year to year. I limited the kill in an effort to make the term *renewable resource* a reality. The last time I hunted those mountains I saw just as many sheep, in the same population composition, as I did the first time there.

Sheep hunting has its own powerful mystique, well recognized, though certainly not fully understood even by the cognoscenti. After my first sheep hunt, one that led me up and down several mountains without my even seeing a sheep, I said never again. But it was already too late. I was hooked. Very soon I found myself on long hikes and climbs searching for white specks, seeking any excuse to be in sheep country any time of the year. The wild ram became my totem.

All hunting perhaps can be explained as a moment when the desire for possession overcomes all other desires. Certainly, people do hunt to own those prized horns and feel the rough curls in their hands. Mere horns, however, do not explain some people's obsession for sheep hunting. There are those who live to hunt sheep. They spend weeks in the hills each autumn searching for a special ram or experience. Many times they pass up opportunities to make a kill. Most times I came home without a ram, not because I couldn't have killed one, but because I didn't find the right ram or circumstance. (Once I encountered a large ram in the lowlands, drinking from a stream, far from his natural terrain. I did not fire a shot. If I'd stalked him for days and found him on a sheer pinnacle, the result would have been different.) I've trekked as much as fifty miles to hunt sheep, and returned content without one. Perhaps it doesn't make much sense.

I often thought the lure was the country itself. Wildlands where clouds snag on peaks and glaciers hang from the sky. Places where the first snow of winter drifts over the painted leaves, muting summer's memory. Places where rams skirmish in the alpenglow, the crash of horns punctuating the symphony of falling water. Where small bands of sheep dot vast landscapes of cloud, rock, water, and sky. Where the air above is perfumed with willow and fireweed, and patches of scarlet bearberry reflect the fire of sun and power of earth.

I can step into it year after year and it seems time has stopped to wait for me. I know where the sheep will be: the rams one place, the lambs and ewes another. The weather might be different—rain, snow, or sun—but nothing really changes. It even seems as if I stalk the same ram I hunted twenty years ago. As I age, I know that the chase doesn't get any easier, it only gets tougher.

Some hunters have deified sheep, imbued rams with supernatural powers. Listening to their stories, you'd think sheep can see through rock and read minds. It isn't the talk of moose or caribou hunters. Sheep hunters are different. They scout for rams weeks before the season. They learn all they can about sheep and donate money to wild sheep conservation groups. They dream about rams with dramatic headgear. The best of them work year-round at physical conditioning. How many people would be willing to carry a hundred-pound backpack of meat, horns, cape, and camp gear for twenty miles? I know people who have. Hewitt used to tell people, "Walker's idea of the ultimate fair-chase hunt is to walk in to the Brooks Range starting from the Fairbanks Airport."

Sheep hunters are very secretive about their favored haunts. When talking to a sheep hunter, never ask where the prized ram came from, unless, of course, you want an honest person to lie. Sheep hunters otherwise are very generous; they'll tell you more about sheep than perhaps you ever cared to know, except for that one thing.

The secrecy is not because of scarcity—on the contrary. An estimated seventy thousand sheep inhabit the Brooks Range, the Chugach, Kenai, Talkeetna and Wrangell mountains, and the magnificent crescent of the Alaska Range, including isolated groups in the White Mountains and Tanana Hills. The numbers, though stable now, have fluctuated throughout this century. According to sketchy records, sheep were very abundant at the turn of the century, but market hunters, who sold the prized meat to miners and construction camps for as little as twenty-five to fifty cents per pound, soon devastated local herds. One of the principal reasons the hunter-naturalist Charles Sheldon lobbied for the establishment of McKinley National Park (now Denali) was to protect sheep from market hunters working for nearby mining interests.

The Alaska Game Law of May 11, 1903 brought some protection to various wildlife. In 1912, the season for Dall sheep was August 1 to December 10, with a bag limit of three sheep. Despite the banning of market hunting in 1925, the decline continued. Predation and the severe winters of 1928–1932 played their parts. By 1949 all of Alaska had been closed to sheep hunting, a result of statewide population estimates of just over 10,000 sheep. In 1954 the season was opened for one month, with the kill limited to rams with three-quarter curl horns or larger. These regulations did not change much until the mid-1970s, when increasing hunting pressure, coupled with improved management techniques, led to the establishment of special limited-access sheep management areas, where for perhaps the first time in Alaska, ethical and aesthetic values took precedence over other factors.

Dall sheep, *Ovis dalli*, named in honor of naturalist William H. Dall, live in the mountains of the Yukon and Northwest territories, Alaska, and northern British Columbia. They are one of four kinds of North American mountain sheep; the Stone sheep of British Columbia and the southern Yukon are a colored subspecies, *Ovis dalli stonei*.

Fossilized evidence indicates the presence of mountain sheep in Alaska as far back as fifty thousand years ago. Of the fifteen forms of mountain sheep worldwide, ours is the only one all-white. The ice and snow of Pleistocene glaciers, which dominated the land when the Dall sheep evolved, appear to account for this camouflaging. But if the white hair is indeed camouflage, why then don't the sheep turn brown in summer, as weasels and snowshoe hares do? Another theory holds that the white pelage of mountain goats and sheep reflects the summer heat, making the shadeless alpine more tolerable.

The real pleasure of professional guiding was showing even a complete greenhorn the ways of the mountains and these wondrous rams, and helping him or her discover and use innate capabilities. The doctrine of our time truly is, as John Steinbeck said, that man can't get along without a whole hell of a lot of stuff. It's almost treason to live in a tent, go hungry, get dirty, and work hard in wet, miserable conditions—for sport!—and expend an excess of time, money, and energy with the very real possibility of returning home with no tangible reward. On a backpack hunt you soon come to appreciate the simplest things, even a temporary haven from wind. You become close to the land and recognize how much excess wealth we accumulate, how many daily luxuries we take for granted. Not all hunters want a backpack hunt—most want horses or aircraft to transport them into the mountains—but many of my hunters took real pride in finding that they could carry a pack, walk more miles in a week than they did in a year at home, and climb mountains at once intimidating and exhilarating.

A guide takes a stranger's welfare into his immediate control. He's responsible for bears, floods, rock slides, bush pilots, and horses; for oatmeal, coffee, and repair tape. Glamour? Say it on the last day of a ten-day hunt that's been washed out by rain and storm.

It may be that people don't need to hunt to experience these things, but camping and photography trips, do not exact the same dues. If the weather gets bad, the camper and the photographer stay inside or go home. On a hunt constrained by time, you go regardless. I can't count the times I've sat shivering in the cold, or been drenched by an icy downpour. Hunters must make the tempo of the natural world their own.

I didn't run a business, as most guides do. I was picky about whom I'd take hunting. Money came second. My candidates had to be interested in more than just killing something. Although I did make a few bad choices, most of my hunters were fine, ethical men and women. The animals we hunted were sought in fair chase, and the kills were earned through hard work. I am proud of the honesty of my guiding career. I tested myself when the real pressure was on—when no one was looking—and measured up.

I decided early on that if I was going to kill a ram, or lead another person to one, it had to be done both lawfully *and* according to my own principles. Hunting for me is not a competition between hunters, or with animals, but rather a self-test. Armed with the latest in optics, gear, clothing, lightweight foods, and modern firearms, the test isn't with animals but an inner test under the constraints of weather and time. I test *me*. The time factor forces me to travel when the weather's bad, climb into fog and wet rock, stay out in the cold and misery of snow, rain, or sleet, and press against the margins of safety.

No one leaps into life with a finely honed set of hunting ethics. In fact, hunting ethics is a new phenomenon precisely because it isn't that long since human beings have stopped hunting out of need. Although I don't think that everyone need abide by my rules, each hunter needs a moral code apart from and above that established by statute. If it is to continue, recreational hunting must be both ethical and responsible. Killing an animal—any animal—should not be a casual occurrence.

Part of sheep hunting's appeal lies precisely in its hardship. Most sheep management areas forbid the use of all-terrain vehicles for hunting, and some even outlaw horses. The elitist view is that mountain hunting is not for everyone and not everyone wanting to hunt sheep should be accommodated. In other words, if you've got the desire and the physical ability, fine; if not, tough.

As in all things, however, there are those who bend or break the rules. Every person who hunts does so for different reasons. Many reasons. Good and bad. Some men do hunt to prove manhood. They need not just risk in business ventures, but physical danger to test courage. On the other hand are those who are willing to buy the illusion of having passed a test of courage.

Aircraft have been misused to spot and herd sheep, to land hunters on mountain ridges above sheep. It is now illegal to hunt the same day a person travels in an airplane, but spotting sheep from the air is still a widespread practice. Rams have even been shot from the air. In the late 1960s, a Dall ram with huge horns was recovered by conservation officers from a ridge above Ship Creek near Anchorage. It had been shotgunned. In the early 1970s an equally giant black-horned ram was found on a ridgetop in the Coal Creek drainage east of the Matanuska River, dead of buckshot wounds.

Violations need not be so blatant to skew the hunt in favor of the hunters. Some guides fire at the same time as the hunter, to ensure nobody goes home empty-handed. For them, the kill, not the seeking and finding, is the centerpiece. I knew one guide who allowed his hunter to shoot three rams before stopping with a heavy-horned ram. Another guide took forty sheep hunters in one year—*forty*—each of whom took home a ram. Such excesses are the inevitable result of competition.

Trophy hunters seek out only the largest rams, the ones that will go in the book. Big money is offered for large rams. Many hunters pay extra for a ram with forty-inch horns, as measured from base to tip along the outer spiral. It is not uncommon for a nine- or ten-year-old ram to have forty-inch horns. But some populations are cropped so hard that few rams live long enough to reach this benchmark. The horns of one Stone ram totalled 101⁶/₈ inches in length, 51⁵/₈ inches on one horn, 50¹/₈ inch on the other. *Almost eight and one half feet of horn.* The largest Dall sheep on record sported one horn in excess of forty-nine inches. A hunter with the late pioneer guide, Morris W. "Slim" Moore, who came to Alaska in 1926, shot a one-horned ram that taped fifty-one inches. He said that another ram he saw moments later had longer horns. Slim died at age eighty-three, thoroughly disgusted with illegal hunters and guides whom he called crop dusters for the way they scoured the hills in their small planes. Many hunters think that the most beautiful of all rams is the one Jonathon Summar killed near the Tok River in 1965. Its horns are 48 and 47 inches and flare out like an Asian argali's. Rams such as these play upon some people's minds. One man had a standing offer of $40,000 for the guide who could guarantee a Dall ram that would place in the records book.

Bucks and books—a combination lethal to ethics. I wish there was no records book. Many hunters have felt the pressure to get into it so strongly that they've ended up hunting for all the wrong reasons. Hunters should not care what standards someone else applies. Some hunters and biologists push for laws that would make only full-curl rams legal game. Thus do they define a trophy. But is a large ram killed on the first day of a hunt while crossing a river bottom more of a trophy than a small ram killed after six days of hard hunting in inclement weather? Size means nothing, yet records keeping honors size only and not the *how*, the quality of the experience. The illegal or unethical procurement of large animals might bolster weak egos, but it debases hunting.

Moreover, the removal of the largest, healthiest rams runs exactly opposite to natural selection, with unknown consequences. If mature rams are shot, then younger rams will be thrust into breeding activities. One biologist foresees a corresponding increase in mortality. Another predicts that the removal of the older, "teaching" animals will result in the loss of "herd knowledge," the memory of routes to winter and summer range. Unproven hypotheses, and yet . . .

On December 2, 1980, ninety-seven million acres of Alaskan land went into new or expanded national parks and refuges. Depending on point of view, the legislation was either the protection of Alaska's wilderness gems or a denial of a way of life, the guarantee of traditional subsistence use or an unnecessary denial of sport hunting. The new 7,952,000-acre Gates of the Arctic National Park and Preserve, and the 12,318,000-acre Wrangells–St. Elias Park and Preserve contain some of the best Dall sheep habitat in the world. Sheep hunting was a thing of the past in these parks and altered forever outside them by the consolidation and concentration of hunting pressure on limited range.

During the battle over the 1980 lands act, many hunters found themselves torn between a desire to protect their heritage, or lose it in order to see the land protected from development. In retrospect one of the greatest blunders hunting organizations made was banding together with developers, miners, and the timber industry to fight against the parklands. The fight pitted hunters against others who, in the clarity of hindsight, desired the same general end: the protection of wildlands for wildlife. All hunters sadly became synonymous with plunderers.

Some of the new parklands excluded hunters unnecessarily. Now it seems that hunters will lose their heritage faster from development, and the misdeeds of some of their own number, than because lands were set aside for wildlife.

The distance between nonhunters and hunters has not closed much. Many nonhunters do not understand how in modern times people can find pleasure in hunting. They want to know how someone can kill what they profess to admire and find beautiful. I have no answer but I recall what a hunter once told me as we sat around a campfire one evening.

"As I straightened up from putting the last skinned quarter in the plastic bag in my pack," he said, "I looked at my bloody hands and knife, at the offal steaming in the early morning light, and thought of the beautiful creature we'd killed and turned into a pile of reeking gore. It shocked me. *My God, I thought, What have we done?*

"But later, here in camp, after the hard work of packing in the meat, and with the ram horns next to the tent, the ribs sizzling by the coals, I relaxed. I thought of the work it took to get here and the obstacles overcome.

"I know that animals die every moment so that other animals might live. I know that in this world only a few do the killing of animals for the many. I know this ram—twelve years old, you said?—has lived a long life and died a better death than starvation. These things I know. But why do I do it? How do I reconcile it?

"I always come back to the stalk: a time when every sense is alert, my mind alive and active, unconscious of any thought other than evaluating sensory perception. It's almost like meditation. Seldom do I concentrate so. I feel every whisper of wind and hear every sound. I'm aware of every muscle in my body and demand precise control as I step from wobbly rock to wobbly rock. In the end is the paradox: close to another creature's death, I feel most alive.

"Sitting here eating this"—with hands dripping meat juice, he waved the thin cut of backstrap charred over a fire—"I think again of the life I have taken to yield this food and those horns. I never think of a living animal when I eat bacon, burgers, or chicken. Never.

"Right now there seems to be no closer return to our primal origins than you and me sitting around this fire, telling stories, and gnawing on these ribs. That's as close as I can come to understanding. But I don't really understand. I just accept it."

I closed my eyes and took a bite of succulent meat. At once I'm on the slope above the rams, stepping as soft as I can so that the sheep will not hear. I sneak close, using as cover every boulder, rise, and gully. I strive for invisibility. I fear this ram's incredible senses and alertness. I see again my partner raise his rifle and I hear the shot, see the ram wince, and fall.

V

Summer, Alaska Range. Mosquitoes attacked us in ferocious assaults and nothing kept them at bay. It was as hot as I'd ever seen it in sheep country, perhaps more than ninety degrees, and instead of T-shirts we wore heavy flannel shirts soaked with bug dope. I twitched constantly as the swarms bit through the repellent and cloth. Still, my partner and I were immeasurably better off than the rams we were watching. Insects ringed their eyes and nostrils and crawled over their soft undersides. Blood oozed through white hair.

In late evening, a breeze finally began to build, giving us all a respite from the insects. We followed the rams out onto a spur of the ridge most exposed to the wind and sat down within comfortable camera range. It had been a harsh winter with heavy snows, and still, in July, the tundra sward was dappled with patchy snow.

Around eleven o'clock, with the sun just going down, we put the tent up. In summer almost twenty hours of daylight energizes the Alaska Range with a pace even human beings find hard to resist. We'd been up since six and following the rams all day, yet we weren't tired, only glad the damn bugs were gone. Once inside the tent, which we put up mostly to keep the bugs away should the wind quit, we lay on our bags watching the light thinning over the hills, the rams feeding in the cooling air.

Sometime after midnight I awoke to the nylon rattling in a stiff wind and the distant roll of thunder. I could see heavy scud drifting over the valley and mountains. As the wind built, the thunder crept closer, and soon far flashes of lightning jabbed the Alaska Range.

The wind shaking the tent woke my partner. He rolled over and looked out to watch the lightning edge across the valley. Soon the storm was directly over us, thunder louder than any I'd ever heard, loud enough to *feel*. To converse over it and the pounding wind, we had to holler. We *Yahooed!* with excitement as multiple bolts of lightning daggered the tundra and mountains.

The wind, the thunder, the lightning more than made up for the earlier travails. Then I had a thought. "Ron," I yelled, "do you know anything about lightning rods?" He started to yell something, then grabbed the tent pole by the door. And just as quickly, I pulled down the back pole.

It seemed then that fire rained to earth terribly close-by. One bolt seemed to strike a mile distant on the southern extension of our ridge. We gathered the flapping tent to us and watched the storm move east. As the front passed and the wind died, huge splatters of rain began to fall. We replaced the tent poles and curled back into our bags as the deluge began. The dry earth responded with the scents of renewed soil, wildflowers, and mountain sheep.

Some hours later I awoke in sunlight and the hum of mosquitoes battering against the netting. I heard a noise nearby and looked out. A short distance away a ram stood staring out over the valley, his damp coat steaming in the gold light. Every now and then he stamped his hindleg in agitation at the mosquitoes biting his underbelly.

Winter, Brooks Range. North of the Arctic Circle, on the slopes where the white sheep live, it is cold and dark. The sun went down before Thanksgiving and will not rise again before early January. It is minus thirty degrees and the windchill stands at minus ninety. The sheep gather in the lee of an escarpment, more interested in one another than the weather. Through mid-December the dominant rams will guard their ewes and attack any lesser rams that challenge them. Always they stay closest to the estrous females, intolerant of the approach even of small lambs. It is the rut—the last days, perhaps, of the oldest rams, as well as the first moments of life of the youngest.

The rams began testing one another back in October, when they gathered in huddles to display headgear. The bigger rams easily intimidated lesser rams, the showy horns enough to establish rank without combat. In the weeks afterward, challenges between equals were settled with charges into head-on combat. Only the strongest, heavy-horned rams control the mating. It is nature's way of selecting the most successful animals, those long-lived enough to achieve dominant status.

Several times I have slogged through snow and climbed onto icy slopes to watch rutting sheep. In winter, they are not hard to find: their tracks show up easily in the right light and they look yellow against the snow. I've seen no more beautiful sight than a band of rams single-filing through new powder. They look so different in their long winter hair. A few rams look as though they weigh four hundred pounds instead of two hundred. Whenever I've sat shivering on a hillside watching the rut, I've wished for such a coat.

It often seems strange to me that their rut comes so late in the year, when stress is already high. The demands placed by cold and snow and minimal rations should be enough without this. The ewes, except when receptive, carry on as normal a life as the rams will allow. But the rams feed little, if at all, during the rut, and stay agitated, running here and there like dervishes, never resting for long.

In minus-thirty-degree weather, with snow to my knees, I once watched two rams slam into one another, then chase several ewes over an icy slope. I saw a raven land on a rock and peer down at the rams' frenzy. I watched the raven groom, then hunker down in his fluffed feathers, settling in for what might become a profitable wait.

VI

I went up to see Spencer recently. It was a long, tiring climb up from the river, through the timber and willows, and up over the cliffs to the ridgetop where his ashes are scattered. He died in a plane crash at the head of Kachemak Bay. I've gone to see him only twice since then. It's a hard scrabble to the top, but that's not the reason I've been so derelict.

In many ways Spencer's death affected me more profoundly than perhaps any other single event. His wasn't the first untimely or violent death I'd experienced: Les Crouse died in the insanity of Vietnam, and I had mourned his loss and shared his widow's and children's sorrow. But when the news came of the airplane crash on the Fox River, and the death of both pilot and passenger, I could not accept it, could not believe it. Dead? At twenty-seven?

We'd met in 1971 on his wedding day, an icefogged, minus-thirty, Fairbanks winter morning. The wedding party was to fly to the lodge where Spencer had worked the summer before and where I would begin work in the spring. Conditions conspired against the plan. First, the hangar doors were frozen tight, sealing the waiting and warmed plane inside. After all else failed, the doors finally yielded when rammed with a truck. Then the fog thickened. More delay. When the fog finally began to thin, there was enough daylight for only one flight. Just pilot Jim Pippin, Spencer, his bride-to-be, one close friend, and the Reverend Davy Crockett made the trip. Despite the turmoil, Spencer's good humor struck a chord. Since we shared many interests, including photography and writing, it was inevitable that we would become friends.

On July 10, 1975, Spencer left Homer at dawn on a goat censusing flight. His first choice for pilot, an experienced, local man, was unavailable that day. In coastal Alaska, when the weather's good, you go. So he went with a second choice. They never came back.

Searchers found the burned wreckage just below the Fox River Glacier. His wife, Randi, was devastated. She would suffer a long time. Friends were distressed. All the old questions plagued us. We tried to make sense of it all. Why did it have to happen? Why now? Why is it always the good ones? All the imponderables.

Spencer was cremated in Soldotna and his ashes taken to Fairbanks, where he'd both studied and worked. His background was mountain sheep. He'd studied their use of mineral licks. As the only game biologist in the Homer office of the Alaska Department of Fish and Game, where the rest of the staff were fisheries scientists, he was to have had the opportunity to study both goats and sheep, as well as other animals.

After the memorial service in Fairbanks, Jim Pippin agreed to fly the ashes to the Brooks Range and scatter them along a ridge overlooking the Dietrich River, a place where Spencer had studied sheep—a place special to him.

Only family and two close friends went on the flight. Almost two hours' flying time north of Fairbanks, Pippin flew over the ridge, picked a spot, and in slow flight, scattered the ashes to the wind and prop wash. He flew the length of the ridge, made a turn, and flew back down, his wheels inches above the rock and gravel: a pilot's tribute to a friend.

After Spencer died, I made a real effort to emulate his character. Be more tolerant of others. Be more caring. Fully realize that life doesn't last forever and lead my days accordingly. Not take too much, especially friends, for granted.

A few years ago I made the climb for the first time. The ridgetop was covered by early snow, broken only by lichen-covered gray rock. Fog obscured the river valley, and only the peaks and ridges floated above the boiling gray. A high overcast blotted the sun. The wind whipping down from the north made the cold real.

This was not what I wanted to see, to experience. On nicer days, from summits to the south, I'd glassed the ridge and thought it looked inviting. I wanted to walk slowly along the crest and look off at the wondrous vistas stretching clear to the Gates of the Arctic, north to Atigun, and east to Chandalar. I wanted to see a ram. I didn't see a living creature.

It was just too much. I wanted the good memories: the laugh, the funny stories of camping trips, the tales of wild sheep. Instead, I was depressed, almost fearful. I worried that the fog would rise and obscure the ridge. I could lose my way, hypothermia become a real threat. I started down.

For a long time I was upset with myself. I know the country; I know that warm summer days are illusory, and cold and snow, reality. But the ridge didn't seem the appropriate place for Spencer. I would think of him and see black and white. Feel cold.

Years went by before I had the time, or desire, to go back. I never really intended to do so. But not long ago, after a sheep hunt, I had the time. The weather was good, the fall colors rioting. So I went.

On top, the air, crisp and still, carried the scent of autumn, of cranberries, blueberries, and moulding leaves. In all directions the peaks stood sharp against a clear sky. Below, the river meandered silver through a patchwork of yellow, red, and green, forest and tundra. It was one of those days when you want to stretch to the tips of your toes and expand your chest and body to take it all in.

I had no idea where the ashes were. I chose to sit on an outcropping with an unlimited panorama of the valley. I faced south, downriver. A golden eagle soared on a thermal. Somewhere ravens talked on the wind.

"Hello, Spence. It's been a long time." I hardly knew what more to say. It seemed odd to say anything. I stopped.

I pictured him wearing his beat-up cowboy hat and fringed buckskin shirt. At heart, he felt he was an old-time mountain man, a hunter and wanderer of far places. He'd stalked animals with a muzzle-loading rifle. Also with a camera and a notebook.

He used to say what seemed back then to be the most provocative things. I remembered a conversation we'd had about a caribou he'd killed on the North Slope. He told how he'd made several trips to pack the meat out. On one trip, perhaps the last, he'd spooked an arctic fox that was feeding on the carcass. As he recalled the moment, he wondered aloud: "Do I have the right to take this meat? Take it from the foxes and wolves to whom it rightly belongs? I thought of leaving the meat for the fox." Such musings about rights and the propriety of hunting struck me then as almost heretical. I wished, now, I could tell Spencer that although it had taken awhile, I finally understood.

Looking down at the river, I thought of the home movies he used to show of this place. One began with a time-lapse sequence of erecting a tent. On the screen was Spencer moving at the speed of a Keystone Kop, the tent flying up. The final sequence, shot at normal speed, showed our smug hero posing by the tightly drawn tent. Another film showed him peering through a giant rip in the bottom of his upturned rubber raft. I laughed outloud.

I sobered, remembering his fear of flying. Sometimes he'd return from a fairly uneventful flight and spend time lying down, recovering from airsickness. Even short trips could undo him. For a biologist, in Alaska, this was a major problem. His response was to learn to fly and become a pilot himself.

At public hearings on hunting seasons and management issues, the debate often turns vitriolic, and personal attacks on biologists are not uncommon. *Bureaucrats. Cushy jobs. College graduates ignorant in the ways of real Alaska, ruining the hunting and wildlife.* Spencer's equanimity with department critics, some of whom were friends, was striking. Yet he knew the truth. A biologist's job is not easy, or particularly safe. On July 27, 1972, his colleague and friend, biologist Jim Erickson, and pilot-biologist Gerald Fisher were killed in a crash while on a sheep survey on the Hulahula River, a drainage not far from where I sat.

Enough was enough. I stood up and walked up the ridge. I came on a caribou antler. Rodents had gnawed off the tips. The antler was aged, rough and porous, sandpapery. One side was bleached white; the other, the down side, was brown. I turned it this way and that, trying to figure its original shape and size. It was impossible to judge how long it had been there. I bent and laid the antler just the way it had fallen, fitting it exactly into the depression in the lichen. I turned to walk away, then froze. To the north, ever so faintly, a wolf howled. I strained to hear. Just then, like the many other times I'd heard howling wolves, I felt acutely alone. Once more the long call swept over the rocks. I hurried north to a cliff and looked down. I waited and waited, but the wolf never howled again.

In a while, out of the corner of my eye I saw movement. Something was walking along the cliff below me and to the right. I hoped it was the wolf. I raised my binoculars and instead saw a Dall ewe, alert and vigilant, leading her lamb quietly along a narrow trail.

I wished I could point them out to someone. Share the discovery. The sheep took a long time to walk around the mountain and out of sight.

That evening, when I climbed down through the cliffs on the way back to camp, the last light of day was on the summits. With the worst of the route behind me, I could slow up. I looked back. Bathed in rich, gold light, the rocks glowed almost with life. But in all too short a time, the alpenglow faded from amber, to red, to white, to nothing.

Now, when I hear that the first winter snows blanket the Brooks Range, a picture of Spencer's ridge comes to mind. I see the cliffs blasted with wind-driven snow.

But, finally, it's all right.

"No wonder the ruined woods I used to know, don't cry out for retribution!" he thought. "The people who have destroyed it will accomplish its revenge."

William Faulkner
Delta Autumn